THE IMPORTANCE OF

Mother Teresa

These and other titles are included in The Importance Of biography series:

Alexander the Great
Muhammad Ali
Maya Angelou
Louis Armstrong
James Baldwin
Clara Barton
The Beatles
Alexander Graham Bell
Napoleon Bonaparte
Julius Caesar
Rachel Carson
Charlie Chaplin
Charlemagne
Cesar Chavez
Winston Churchill
Cleopatra
Christopher Columbus
Hernando Cortes
Marie Curie
Charles Dickens
Emily Dickinson
Walt Disney
Amelia Earhart
Thomas Edison
Albert Einstein
Duke Ellington
F. Scott Fitzgerald
Dian Fossey
Anne Frank
Benjamin Franklin
Galileo Galilei
Emma Goldman
Jane Goodall
Martha Graham
Lorraine Hansberry
Stephen Hawking
Ernest Hemingway
Jim Henson
Adolf Hitler

Harry Houdini
Thomas Jefferson
Mother Jones
Chief Joseph
John F. Kennedy
Martin Luther King Jr.
Joe Louis
Douglas MacArthur
Malcolm X
Thurgood Marshall
Margaret Mead
Golda Meir
Michelangelo
Wolfgang Amadeus
Mozart
John Muir
Sir Isaac Newton
Richard M. Nixon
Georgia O'Keeffe
Louis Pasteur
Pablo Picasso
Elvis Presley
Jackie Robinson
Norman Rockwell
Eleanor Roosevelt
Anwar Sadat
Margaret Sanger
Oskar Schindler
William Shakespeare
John Steinbeck
Tecumseh
Mother Teresa
Jim Thorpe
Mark Twain
Queen Victoria
Pancho Villa
Leonardo da Vinci
H. G. Wells
Simon Weisenthal

THE IMPORTANCE OF

Mother Teresa

by Rafael Tilton

Lucent Books, P.O. Box 289011, San Diego, CA 92198-9011

Library of Congress Cataloging-in-Publication Data

Tilton, Rafael.
    Mother Teresa / by Rafael Tilton.
        p.   cm.—(The importance of)
    Includes bibliographical references and index.
    Summary: A biography of the nun who founded the order
known as the Missionaries of Charity to work with the sick
and destitute in Calcutta and other places and who was
awarded the Nobel Peace Prize in 1979.
    ISBN 1-56006-565-6 (lib. bdg. : alk. paper)
    1. Teresa, Mother, 1910–1997—Juvenile literature.
    2. Missionaries of Charity—Biography—Juvenile
literature. [1. Teresa, Mother, 1910–1997. 2. Nuns. 3. Missionaries of Charity.   4. Women—Biography. 5. Nobel Prizes
Biography]   I. Title.   II. Series.
BX4406.5.Z8T55   2000
271'.97—dc21   99–35395
    [B]   CIP

Copyright 2000 by Lucent Books, Inc., P.O. Box 289011,
San Diego, California 92198-9011

Printed in the U.S.A.

Contents

Foreword   7

Important Dates in the Life of Mother Teresa   8

INTRODUCTION
Everyone's Peacemaker   10

CHAPTER 1
A Happy Family in the Eye of a Storm (1910–1928)   13

CHAPTER 2
Behind Cloister Walls in Calcutta (1928–1946)   23

CHAPTER 3
Testing a New Calling (1946–1960)   36

CHAPTER 4
*Expanding the Ministry to the
Unwanted (1960–1970)*   54

CHAPTER 5
Boundary Crossings (1970–1979)   66

CHAPTER 6
A Peacemaker Above Politics (1979–1991)   83

CHAPTER 7
"She Was Tough" (1991–1997)   96

EPILOGUE
The Legacy   106

Notes   111

For Further Reading   115

Works Consulted   117

Index   121

Picture Credits   127

About the Author   128

Foreword

THE IMPORTANCE OF biography series deals with individuals who have made a unique contribution to history. The editors of the series have deliberately chosen to cast a wide net and include people from all fields of endeavor. Individuals from politics, music, art, literature, philosophy, science, sports, and religion are all represented. In addition, the editors did not restrict the series to individuals whose accomplishments have helped change the course of history. Of necessity, this criterion would have eliminated many whose contribution was great, though limited. Charles Darwin, for example, was responsible for radically altering the scientific view of the natural history of the world. His achievements continue to impact the study of science today. Others, such as Chief Joseph of the Nez Percé, played a pivotal role in the history of their own people. While Joseph's influence does not extend much beyond the Nez Percé, his nonviolent resistance to white expansion and his continuing role in protecting his tribe and his homeland remain an inspiration to all.

These biographies are more than factual chronicles. Each volume attempts to emphasize an individual's contributions both in his or her own time and for posterity. For example, the voyages of Christopher Columbus opened the way to European colonization of the New World. Unquestionably, his encounter with the New World brought monumental changes to both Europe and the Americas in his day. Today, however, the broader impact of Columbus's voyages is being critically scrutinized. *Christopher Columbus*, as well as every biography in The Importance Of series, includes and evaluates the most recent scholarship available on each subject.

Each author includes a wide variety of primary and secondary source quotations to document and substantiate his or her work. All quotes are footnoted to show readers exactly how and where biographers derive their information, as well as provide stepping stones to further research. These quotations enliven the text by giving readers eyewitness views of the life and times of each individual covered in The Importance Of series.

Finally, each volume is enhanced by photographs, bibliographies, chronologies, and comprehensive indexes. For both the casual reader and the student engaged in research, The Importance Of biographies will be a fascinating adventure into the lives of people who have helped shape humanity's past and present, and who will continue to shape its future.

Important Dates in the Life of Mother Teresa

1910
Agnes Gonxha Bojaxhiu, the youngest of three children, is born in Skopje in the modern-day Republic of Macedonia on August 26.

1929
Enters novitiate in Darjeeling, India, on May 23.

1937
Professes final vows and accepts the rule of enclosure as Mother Teresa on May 24. Continues to teach geography to middle-class Bengali girls.

1949
Moves into the Gomes home in February; first postulant, Subhasini Das, arrives on March 19.

1950
Missionaries of Charity constitutions are approved for Mother Teresa and ten sisters on October 7.

1910	1920	1930	1940	1950	1960

1919
Nikola Bojaxhiu, her father, dies.

1928
Agnes travels from Skopje to Rathfarnham, Ireland, to join the Sisters of Loreto.

1946
On September 10, while on a train to Darjeeling for a retreat, she hears a new call to minister in the streets of Calcutta.

1959–1960
Order approved for spread throughout India.

1931
On May 24 professes first vows and is sent on a mission, first to Bengal, then to Loreto Entally in Calcutta as a teacher of geography with outreach to St. Teresa's parish school.

1948
On August 18 begins her year of exclaustration wearing a white sari with a blue border; goes to Patna for medical training; begins her street ministry in Calcutta slum, Moti Jihl, on December 21; becomes an Indian citizen.

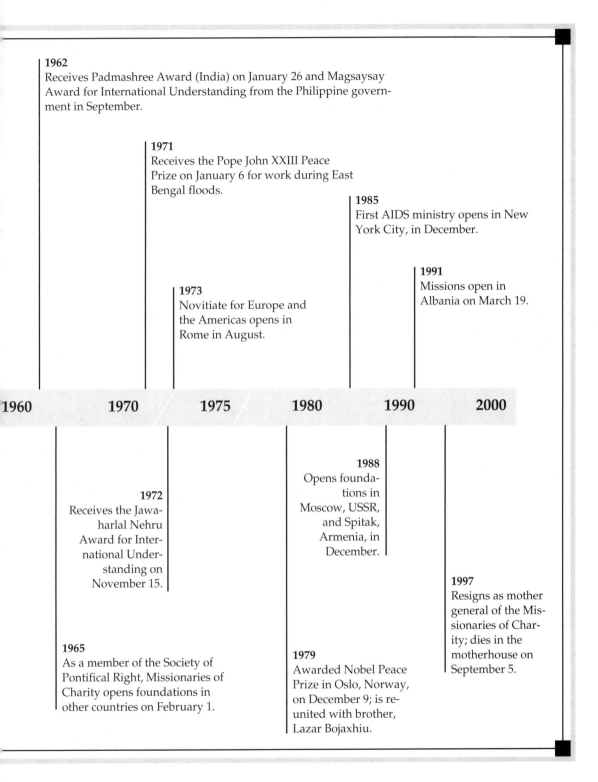

1962
Receives Padmashree Award (India) on January 26 and Magsaysay Award for International Understanding from the Philippine government in September.

1971
Receives the Pope John XXIII Peace Prize on January 6 for work during East Bengal floods.

1985
First AIDS ministry opens in New York City, in December.

1991
Missions open in Albania on March 19.

1973
Novitiate for Europe and the Americas opens in Rome in August.

1960	1970	1975	1980	1990	2000

1988
Opens foundations in Moscow, USSR, and Spitak, Armenia, in December.

1972
Receives the Jawaharlal Nehru Award for International Understanding on November 15.

1997
Resigns as mother general of the Missionaries of Charity; dies in the motherhouse on September 5.

1965
As a member of the Society of Pontifical Right, Missionaries of Charity opens foundations in other countries on February 1.

1979
Awarded Nobel Peace Prize in Oslo, Norway, on December 9; is reunited with brother, Lazar Bojaxhiu.

Everyone's Peacemaker

Mother Teresa of Calcutta, the former head of the Missionaries of Charity, who ministered to the poorest of the poor in Calcutta, India, in some ways seems an unlikely person to receive the Nobel Peace Prize. In her daily life she was so ordinary, so much like anyone else. She did not see herself as special or as deserving public acclaim. Yet, unbidden fame followed her. Says her biographer Kathryn Spink, "Her life was public property, and . . . public attention . . . would pursue her relentlessly to the end of her days."[1]

Mother Teresa used that attention to point out that the hungry, outcast, homeless, diseased, and dying are everywhere. They are found in every country and in every walk of life. Moreover, she believed that not only are the poorest of the poor hungry for love, the ministers to the poor are themselves outcast until they learn to love and be loved.

Mother Teresa believed that the importance of her work was separate from its social impact. She and the Missionaries of Charity do only religious work, she once said. Whether running homes for abandoned children, lepers, and the destitute

Mother Teresa's lifelong dedication to serving the poorest of the poor earned her the Nobel Peace Prize and the admiration of millions of people around the world.

and dying in India or ministering to drug addicts and AIDS patients in the United States, they are loving God "in distressing disguise."[2] This, she felt, made their work different from that of social agencies like the Red Cross or the UN peacekeepers or the Peace Corps workers. Although the Missionaries of Charity and secular workers all assist in natural and man-made disasters, helping tenderly and lovingly, it was doing it for Jesus, she believed, that made her work different.

Mother Teresa appealed to people to make direct contact with the ones they serve. By serving the poorest of the poor, she said, people experience the most fulfilling love. The only way to prove this unlikely idea, she believed, is to try it. Many people accepted her challenge, and her importance grew as a result.

As winner of the Nobel Peace Prize, Mother Teresa sent an invitation to spread peace by tending the victims of violence. When the Swedish Academy, which awards the Nobel Prize, picked her as someone who advanced the cause of world peace, it was because her unconditionally loving service spoke against violence.

Will Mother Teresa's work last into the twenty-first century? Already there is religious persecution in her adopted

STREET PEOPLE HELPING STREET PEOPLE

In A Simple Path, *compiled by Lucinda Vardey, Missionary of Charity sister Charmaine José describes the work of her order.*

"We are street people and our work is in the streets. We pray as we walk, going out to visit families, to be with a dying child, or to bring medicine to those in need. Each sister takes one street a day to see what help we can give the poor. We also go out to the villages where there are hardly any facilities and we open medical centers there. Sometimes we take care of 2,500 patients a week in these places."

A sister from Mother Teresa's order teaches poor children at a mission in the Mexican city of Tijuana. The Missionaries of Charity do much of their work in the streets, where they seek out the neediest people.

homeland, India. Missionaries of Charity have been kidnapped and killed in Sierra Leone. Fighting in Kosovo, near where she grew up, has intensified to the point of intervention by world powers. But there is strong evidence of perseverance among those who are drawn to the Missionaries of Charity, young and old, members and coworkers. Daily those who follow in Mother Teresa's footsteps are reaching out to the world's poorest individuals.

Chapter

1 A Happy Family in the Eye of a Storm (1910–1928)

Agnes Gonxha (GOHN-ja) Bojaxhiu (BOY-ya-jee-oo) was born in the town of Skopje (SKO-pee-ay), in the modern-day Republic of Macedonia, which was then a principality ruled by the Ottoman Turks and located in the southeastern corner of Europe, north of modern-day Greece. By the late 1800s several principalities, notably Serbia and Bulgaria, had won their independence from Turkey, and many nationalistic Slavic people of this area, called the Balkans, were hoping to add Macedonia to a growing alliance of Slavic states.

The region was a mixture of ethnic and religious groups. Agnes's parents, Nikola and Drana Bojaxhiu, were not themselves Slavic but Albanian. In Skopje, a city of about twenty-five thousand on the Vardar River, the Bojaxhius and a small number of other Albanians of the Sacred Heart Church parish were both an ethnic and religious minority. They were Roman Catholics, politically more aligned with Roman Catholic Croatians in the area than to their more numerous Albanian countrymen who had converted to Islam. Moreover, Skopje was up to 60 percent populated by Eastern Orthodox Slavic Serbs.

When they were first married around 1900, the Bojaxhius lived in Prizren, then the capital of Kosovo, in Serbia. Soon after their marriage, they moved fifty miles south to Skopje, where Nikola opened a grocery business. It was there that they started their family. Their first daughter, Aga, was born in 1904; their son, Lazar, was born in 1907.

Mother Teresa was born Agnes Gonxha Bojaxhiu in 1910 in the town of Skopje, Macedonia (pictured here in 1974).

Nikola soon teamed up with a friend who was a building contractor. With his partner, he built the Skopje Theater and became prosperous enough to own two houses. He expanded his grocery business by importing commodities such as fruits from the Mediterranean. Fluent in Italian, French, Serbo-Croatian, Turkish, and his native Albanian, Nikola took naturally to the wide travel required for his work. He also entered public life in Skopje, serving as a town councilman. Publicly loyal to the Turkish overlords, in private he was sympathetic with Albanian nationalists. This militant group hoped to add the fertile agricultural area of Kosovo, with its Albanian majority, to a Greater Albania.

Nikola's son, Lazar, remembers his father this way: "He was full of life and liked to be with people. Our house was full of visitors while he was alive. They talked a lot about politics. He told us never to forget whose children we were and from what background we came."[3]

Agnes's mother, Dranafile Bernai, a name usually shortened to Drana (DRAH-na, meaning "rose"), traced her ancestry to Palermo on the island of Sicily, a stronghold of immigrant Albanian Roman Catholics. Drana strongly defended her family's religious identity, as shown by their affectionate name for her: Nana Loka, or "Mother of the Soul."

By the time Agnes was born on August 26, 1910, the Bojaxhiu family was living in a roomy, modern house surrounded by a garden, flower beds, and fruit trees. Her brother, Lazar, who was three years old when she was born, remembered that the family thought of Agnes "as a rosebud," a perception that accounted for her middle name, Gonxha, meaning "rosebud." Speaking almost seventy years later with biographer Eileen Egan, he recalled:

> When she was a child, she was plump, round, and tidy. She was sensible and a little too serious for her age. Of the three of us, she was the one who did not steal the jam. However, being generous and kindhearted, she would help me in the dining room to pull open the drawer of the cupboard high up against the wall because I could not manage it myself.[4]

THE SURROUNDING STORM

Political events during Agnes's early years were swirling around Macedonia. When she was barely two, Montenegro, Bulgaria, Greece, and Serbia declared war on Turkey. In the three months of what later came to be known as the First Balkan War, fighting reached as far south as Skopje. When representatives of these countries, known as the Balkan League, met with the leaders of Turkey in London on December 3, 1912, their peace treaty terms placed Skopje on the new western border of Serbia.

Peace was short-lived. Within a month, the Second Balkan War was on, with Serbia's former ally, Bulgaria, now objecting to the peace terms. Before Agnes's third birthday, following the Treaty of Bucharest

AGNES AND HER MOTHER

To biographer Lush Gjergji, Lazar Bojaxhiu related many stories of Agnes's early life, including this analysis of her character and personality, which was quoted in Mother Teresa: Her Life, Her Works.

"She was a normal girl, perhaps a bit shy and introverted. She had many friends, and spent much time with them, for they often visited her. Already in elementary school she showed her inclination for study. She was first in her class, ever ready to help others. I remember that she had a close friend, the daughter of a doctor. Even as a small girl she had a gift for poetry, and wrote some poems and read them to her companions. With them she was very open, whereas with men she was more reserved. However, she was very sociable, and paid no attention to others' religion, tongue, or nationality. I never heard her say no to her parents. Mamma often told me: 'Do like Agnes, even if she is smaller than you.'

Mother always insisted on order and discipline among us. Every night the three of us, Aga, Agnes and I, in turn, had to polish our shoes. Many times I would ask her, 'Agnes, do it for me, please' and she would answer, 'all right, little brother, I will.' If I had some mischief up my sleeve and she found out about it, she never played the spy. As far as I know, I believe mother felt that Agnes had a religious vocation. I recall that she sometimes said that we would not have long to enjoy Agnes' company, for two reasons: either because of her frail health, or because she would give herself to God. Mother loved Agnes very much, but when God called her, mother offered her to him willingly."

on August 10, 1913, northern Macedonia, including Skopje, and all of Kosovo belonged to Slavic Serbia.

Again peace proved elusive. Less than nine months later, on June 28, 1914, a Serbian rebel named Gavrilo Princip assassinated Archduke Francis Ferdinand, the designated heir to the Austro-Hungarian throne, touching off World War I. Thus, before Agnes was four, Serbia was once again at war, this time with Austria-Hungary.

World War I quickly engulfed Europe, with battle fronts all around Skopje. At the end of the war, the Treaty of Versailles

THE BALKAN WARS

RUSSIA

AUSTRIA-HUNGARY

BOSNIA
Sarajevo •
HERZEGOVINA

SERBIA

ROMANIA
Bucharest •

MONTENEGRO

• Sofia

BULGARIA

• Prizren

ITALY   • Tiranë   THRACE
ALBANIA   Constantinople •

MACEDONIA

CORFU   GREECE

OTTOMAN
EMPIRE

• Athens

Ionian
Sea

- - - - Boundary of the Ottoman Empire in 1912
before the Balkan Wars

Territory lost by the Ottoman Empire during
the Balkan Wars, 1912–1913

THE EYE OF THE STORM

During the war years, at least for Agnes, family and the church community seemed like a pocket of calm and happiness. The three children accompanied their mother, Drana, down the block to Sacred Heart Church, the center of their parish, for daily mass in the morning. They attended the parish elementary school, where they learned about their religion and how to read and write the Albanian language. Nikola came home from work nearly every night to a family meal lovingly prepared by his wife.

Both Nikola and Drana devoted themselves to the works of mercy and involved their children as well. Agnes often went with her mother to take food and money to homes of the poor. Other poor people who came to their door asking for help must have been refugees from the war-

A Serbian rebel is arrested following his assassination of Archduke Francis Ferdinand, the incident that started World War I.

awarded Agnes's hometown to yet another nation, Yugoslavia, encompassing several Balkan states and provinces, each with highly different aims and allegiances.

The political turmoil that had changed the name of their homeland could hardly have been a reality to Agnes in those years. In 1918, when World War I was over, she was only eight. When asked about her early life by her biographers, she would merely say it was happy but she was reluctant to talk about it.

torn areas of nearby Kosovo. Nikola and Drana, who were strongly committed to a centuries-old Albanian tradition of *besa*, "hospitality," saw the poor as having a claim on their help. Nikola always reserved enough money at home for Drana to give them in their need. They might be invited in for a meal or even provided with shelter. As biographer Egan writes, "When the children asked who the people were, [Drana] would tell them that the needy were part of their family too. Poor people learned that they would not be turned away from the Bojaxhiu door."[5]

Helping the poor in their homes could be risky in times of war. Egan explains that the spirit of Albanian hospitality meant that,

> should a family promise hospitality to someone and he came to claim it, the family would provide it and protect that person at any cost. The cost might be heavy indeed if the person claiming hospitality were, as often happened, a hunted man stalked by seekers after retribution or vengeance. The pledge would be fulfilled even in the extreme situation that word came that the guest had been involved in the death of a member of the host family.[6]

To Agnes, it seemed that the happiness of the Bojaxhius came from her parents' taking seriously the values of love and charity. They drew closer by helping strangers, entertaining visitors, and appreciating life. Meanwhile, her father continued active involvement in the movement to join Kosovo to Greater Albania—

involvement that was about to drastically transform their family life.

TRAGIC AND SUDDEN DEATH

In 1919, when Agnes was nearly nine years old, Nikola traveled the 165 miles to Belgrade to attend a political dinner with representatives of other nationalistic groups interested in winning Kosovo for Albanians. When he had left home he was forty-five, healthy, enthusiastic, and dynamic, but when he returned he was violently ill with internal bleeding.

Seeing how sick Nikola was, Drana immediately sent Agnes for the parish priest. When the child could not find him at the parish rectory, she went to the railway station where she saw a traveling priest waiting for the train. She begged him to come minister to her father, and he agreed.

Nikola was clearly dying. The family joined the priest in praying as he administered the last rites. Then the bleeding man was taken to the hospital. The doctors could not save his life, and he never returned home. Although no firm evidence exists, circumstances and the attempted treatments and surgery performed suggest that he might have been poisoned. Who the perpetrators were or what their motives might have been is similarly unknown.

The effects on the Bojaxhiu family of Nikola's sudden death were just as sudden and decisive. His business partner took over all of the business assets, leaving the family without means of support.

And Drana, filled with grief, retreated to her bedroom for several months, leaving Agnes's older sister, Aga, who was then scarcely fifteen years old, all of the household responsibilities.

A New Life for the Bojaxhiu Family

Once Drana came to terms with the death of her husband, she again devoted herself to the care of her family. Her achievement in keeping the family together remained, for Agnes, of primary importance: "We were all very united," she said in later life, "especially after the death of my father. We lived for each other and we made every effort to make one another happy. We were a very united and a very happy family."[7]

Drana turned to a business of her own to support herself and her children. Her decision to sell clothing and handcrafted fabric rested on her skill in embroidery and lace making. Her business soon expanded to include the sale of woven wool rugs, for which Skopje was famous. Her son, Lazar, recalled later that when he accompanied her on business visits, he saw that managers of the textile factories knew the value of her advice on the most popular designs and materials.

School and Religion Are Separated

Agnes soon completed the four grades offered at the parish's elementary school and went on to high school at the secular Serbo-Croatian Gymnasium. Religious training, however, continued at home in the form of catechism (lessons on Catholic beliefs) and prayer. Drana's two consuming concerns were her children and her religion. Every evening the family would gather for twenty minutes or so to recite the Hail Mary prayer fifty times, keeping track on the rosary beads while they meditated on the life of Jesus.

Drana also took time for pilgrimages. A favorite pilgrimage took the family to the shrine of the Madonna of Letnice located north of Skopje. There, Drana prayed especially for Agnes, who seemed to be physically weak. Worried by Agnes's recurring cough, she arranged to have Agnes herself devote two separate pilgrimages of her own to pray for good health.

In this atmosphere, it was natural for Agnes to consider devoting her life to acts of mercy. Asked later by an interviewer about when she had first decided to dedicate herself to the service of God, she said it was in 1922: "I was only twelve years old then. . . . [W]e children used to go to a non-Catholic school but we also had very good priests who were helping the boys and the girls to follow their vocation according to the call of God."[8]

According to Lazar, the parish took a good deal of the family's attention. He commented in an interview,

> We lived next to the parish church of the Sacred Heart of Jesus. Sometimes my mother and sisters seemed to live as much in the church as they did at

A Religious Center in the Home

In his biography Teresa of Calcutta, *Robert Serrou includes a long letter written by Agnes's brother, Lazar, in which he recounts some of his early memories.*

"Where our house had been a hotbed of political discussion while my father lived, after his death it was more of a religious center. And this shows you how Teresa became Teresa: why she became a nun in the first place. Our mother was unusually religious, the girls were always organizing church activities and choir singing, and we constantly tried to help people. My mother was interested in missions, and she would take in local people too and feed and help them.

I remember when my mother found out about a poor woman in Skopje who had a tumor and had no one to care for her. Her family refused to help or even to give her shelter. My mother brought this woman to live in our house. With all her other responsibilities, my mother housed and fed the woman and cared for her until she got well. So you see, 'Teresa' did not just spring out of the blue.

Gonxha [Agnes], by age thirteen, when I left home, was already fascinated by mission work. She loved to meet returning missionaries and hear their accounts of work in the field. She seemed to remember every detail. Once, at a church meeting when Gonxha was twelve or thirteen, our new parish priest, a Jesuit, showed a map of the world with missions indicated on it. Gonxha amazed everyone by going up to the map and explaining the activities and exact location of every one of the missions."

home. They were always involved with the choir, the religious services, and missionary topics.[9]

There was discipline as well. Agnes later recalled that Drana once made a strong point of calling her family to self-denial by turning off the electric lights on some silly and bantering talk: "She told us that there was no use wasting electricity so that such foolishness could go on."[10]

Agnes in particular was drawn to Drana's severe simplicity. To Lazar, Agnes was like their mother, "so strong, so strict in religious practice."[11] A family photograph taken when Agnes was a teenager shows that she also looked like her mother, having a long, slender, oval face, a large nose, and a small frame and bone structure.

Agnes's community contributions during her high school years included joining twenty other young people in the Albanian Catholic Choir of Skopje, singing solos, and helping with plays and skits at Christmas and other religious holidays. Despite deep involvement in her parish church's activities, her early desire for a religious vocation faded. Lazar, now in military school in Austria, would come home on vacations always to find his sisters involved in their church, in their studies at the gymnasium, or tutoring their companions and thinking happily about their future families.

A GLIMPSE OF THE WORLD BEYOND SKOPJE

Agnes was not, however, inclined to be content with a sheltered life in Skopje. In 1925, when she was fifteen, Agnes began to develop her interest in reading. The new pastor of Sacred Heart Church, a Croatian Jesuit named Father Franjo Jambrenovic, established a parish library. Father Jambrenovic was linked to the cultural and literary communities of Europe, so he included contemporary literature in the library along with spiritual readings. Agnes became an avid reader and was soon engrossed in the novels of Fyodor Dotoyev-sky, idealizing the nationalistic destiny of the Slavic peoples, and Henryk Sienkiewicz's *Quo Vadis?*, which discusses the persecution of Christians by the Roman emperor Nero, as well as Sienkiewicz's other historical novels about the liberation of Poland from foreign domination.

Father Jambrenovic also started a chapter of the Sodality of the Blessed Virgin Mary in his parish. This organization of adolescents and young adults was devoted to challenging young people to go on pilgrimages, help the poor, and learn about the lives of saints and missionaries, along with enjoying nature walks and other social gatherings.

In the sodality's educational sessions, Agnes learned that some Croatian Jesuits

As a teenager, Agnes read the novels of Fyodor Dostoyevsky (pictured), which idealized the nationalistic destiny of the Slavic peoples.

Agnes became interested in the idea of serving the poor after learning about the work of Jesuit missionaries in impoverished Bengal, India (above).

from Yugoslavia had recently gone on a mission to Bengal, India. Called there in 1924 by Archbishop Ferdinand Perier of Calcutta, they had joined other missionaries in helping the poor and educating them.

The Croatian missionaries wrote home of their work in this poverty-stricken, heavily populated, tropical city north of the Bay of Bengal. They asked their fellow Jesuits to tell others of their needs and difficulties. Father Jambrenovic became enthusiastic about promoting the work of his fellow Croatian priests and communicated that enthusiasm to Agnes.

The strong impression the Jesuits' letters made on Agnes is indicated by an incident recounted later by her cousin Lorenc Antoni, from whom she took mandolin lessons. In 1927, when Agnes was seventeen, she wanted to pay Antoni for her lessons. Upon his refusal, she told him, "Take it and give it to me for the missions in India."[12]

As she worked with the sodality, Agnes became more and more interested in the work of the missionaries in India. She joined a group that prayed for missions around the world. Still, she did not want to be a missionary herself, but to have a family. She was satisfied to think of her daily experience in a sacrificing, religious home as close to the ideals expressed in the letters from foreign lands.

WANTING THE UNWANTED

But the idea of service continued to draw Agnes. Between 1927 and 1928, Agnes made two more pilgrimages to the shrine of the Madonna of Letnice; while there, she tried to reconcile the growing conflict between her hopes of having a family of her own and her unbidden urge to go to the missions. One of these retreats was on the Feast of the Assumption of Mary, August 15, 1928. After this pilgrimage to the shrine, Agnes's desire to serve God among the faraway Bengali people intensified.

From the letters of the Croatian Jesuits, Agnes learned of the Sisters of Loreto, who also served in Bengal. This international order of nuns provided a means for Catholic women to enter mission works. Despite her dreams of raising a family, Agnes made a momentous decision and wrote to the sis-

ters. Years later she spoke of her decision: "At eighteen years of age I decided to leave my home and enter the Sisters of Our Lady of Loreto. Since then I have never had the least doubt that I was right."[13]

When Agnes told her mother that she had decided to become a missionary, Drana was overwhelmed with the thought of separation from her daughter. As Agnes later said, "[We] were very closely united, especially after my father's death. . . . I was very close to my mother."[14] But within a day Drana had accepted the fact of Agnes's vocation and gave her advice that she always remembered: "Put your hand in His—in His hand—and walk all the way with Him."[15]

Through correspondence with the Sisters of Loreto, officially known as the Institute of the Blessed Virgin Mary, Agnes found that their outreach to Bengal was actually based in Rathfarnham, Ireland. Loreto, she learned, was a strict order, and there would be no turning back. Once Agnes entered, she would not visit her family home again.

2 Behind Cloister Walls in Calcutta (1928–1946)

Agnes's mother, Drana, faced her daughter's resolve to be a missionary with characteristic strength. Agnes always remembered her mother's words of encouragement: "When you take on a task, do it willingly, otherwise, do not accept it."[16] And Agnes, for her part, took her orders from God in the Albanian spirit of *besa*: One's word, once given, must never be forsaken.

Although it might seem that she gave up much to join the Sisters of Loreto, in later years Agnes spoke of the gift she had received in return—the joy she experienced in her decision. She recalled a test of her vocation shown to her by Father Jambrenovic:

> If you are glad at the thought that God may be calling you to serve him and your neighbor, this may well be the best proof of your vocation. A deep joy is like the compass which points out the proper direction for your life. One should follow this, even when one is venturing upon a difficult path.[17]

Agnes's decision to be a missionary would mean a great loss to the Sacred Heart Church parish. But after shedding their first tears at the thought of Agnes's going so far away, members organized a special Easter celebration in her honor. During a program of good-bye messages, they offered gifts of things like soap and scarves that she could use on the long trip to Ireland.

Her Albanian biographer Lush Gjergji, who knew her relatives, tells of her last night in Skopje:

> When the time finally came for her to leave, in the evening all the young people of the parish gathered to speak, to sing, and to spend a few last hours together, in Drana Bojaxhiu's house. It was a memorable gathering for all, and a sad one especially for Agnes' mother.[18]

No doubt remained. Agnes had been accepted into the Congregation of the Sisters of the Blessed Virgin Mary of Loreto, who worked as missionaries in India. All was ready for the long trip.

On the Way to a Far Country

Drana and Aga joined Agnes for the first leg of the journey. The train took them north through Kachina, a narrow

GOOD-BYE TO SKOPJE

A diary entry written by Agnes's cousin Lorenc Antoni and quoted in Lush Gjergji's biography Mother Teresa: Her Life, Her Works, *tells of Agnes's departure from Skopje.*

"That evening, September 25, 1928, all of us were gathered in Agnes' house to say goodbye. All brought her some little gift: one a pencil, another a book, or something of the sort, as a souvenir or a 'thank you' token. I gave her a gold fountain pen which she used for a long time. The next day, September 26, was departure day. Many people had come to accompany her: babies, children, almost the entire parish, and her schoolmates as well. All eyes were on her, eyes full of questions and unexpressed doubts; what will become of this girl who is leaving for India, a strange and distant land?

I woke up early. First, I went to church, and thence to the station. I bought three tickets to Zagreb, for Drana, Aga and Agnes. All of them were weeping at the station, even though a few minutes earlier they had all said they would not cry. I came close to crying myself, thinking that I was losing a relative and a dear friend. As we said goodbye she pressed my hand tightly. I replied rather coldly, to help her overcome the sorrow of this moment. The train pulled out; from the quayside all of us waved our handkerchiefs. She kept on waving until she was lost to sight. The sun illuminated her with its rays; she seemed like the moon which gradually vanishes in the brightness of the dawning day. She finally became an ever diminishing point, still waving, but growing fainter and fainter. Finally she disappeared entirely. Nothing more could be seen; it was like a star vanishing in the blaze of the morning sun."

mountain pass, into Kosovo, Serbia, and on into Croatia, where she stayed two weeks in the capital, Zagreb. There she made contact with a publication of the Pontifical Society for the Propagation of the Faith. Later in 1928 the publication, entitled *Catholic Missions*, carried a notice that indicated the loss Agnes's departure represented for her parish:

Agnes Bojaxhiu is an Albanian, born at Skopje. The Lord's call came to her in high school. Just as St. Peter left his nets behind, so did Agnes leave her books behind and departed in God's name. This amazed everybody because she had been the first in her class and was much esteemed by all. She was the soul of the women's Catholic activities, and of the church choir. All felt that with her departure a vacancy would be created.[19]

On October 13, 1928, she said a last good-bye to her mother and sister and resumed her long train trip. She and a new companion, Betika Kajnc (KANK), who also was answering the call to Loreto, crossed Austria, Switzerland, and France, finally arriving in Paris.

One of the Yugoslav Jesuits had arranged for the young women to be met at the station in Paris by Mother Eugene MacAvin of Loreto House Auteuil, which was located near Paris. After an interview conducted with the aid of an interpreter supplied by the Yugoslav embassy, the two young women were sent on to Loreto Abbey in Rathfarnham, County Dublin, Ireland.

FIRST LESSONS

At Rathfarnham, Agnes and Betika joined other young women (called postulants) who were asking to join the Sisters of Loreto in the novitiate (house where novices are trained) at Rathfarnham. Their tutor was Mother M. Borgia Irwin, a veteran of the mission in India, who supervised their first task: learning English.

After just a few weeks, in mid-November 1928, Agnes and Betika boarded a ship to India. Agnes's inherent toughness helped to sustain her on the journey. Their passage took them through the Suez Canal, the Red Sea, the Indian Ocean, and around the tip of India, finally bringing them to Calcutta, nearly seven weeks later, on January 6, 1929.

THE NOVITIATE AT THE FOOT OF THE HIMALAYAS

India was new to Agnes, but not to her order. The Sisters of Loreto had worked in India since 1841. In Calcutta they ran Loreto House, an exclusive English school where many well-off Indians, both Hindu and Muslim, were educated. The Loreto novitiate, on the other hand, was in Darjeeling, a resort town 450 miles north of Calcutta, 7,000 feet up into the Himalayas. It was to this secluded convent that Agnes and Betika now went by train for their two-year novitiate. There, they would study the life and works of Jesus and learn the skills of teaching in addition to studying English, Hindi, and Bengali.

When they formally entered the novitiate on May 23, 1929, they put on white veils, received their crosses, and formally became known by new names. Betika was now Sister Mary Magdalene. Agnes became known as Sister Teresa.

Agnes, now Sister Teresa, wholeheartedly devoted herself to religious life. In a

At the age of eighteen, Agnes joined the Sisters of Loreto convent in Darjeeling (pictured), a small secluded town in the Himalayas.

letter to her aunt, she told of her happiness on the day of her reception into the novitiate: "Dear Aunt: I am well and my health is good. I am sending you this photo [in white veil] in souvenir of the greatest day of my life, in which I became all Christ's. All my love, from your Agnes, little Teresa of the Child Jesus."[20]

The sisters' first year in the novitiate was almost totally separated from life in the town around them. In the second year they took up studies leading to their apostolate (assigned work) as teachers, including working directly with local children. Sister M. Thérèse Breen, also a novice with Sister Teresa, later recalled:

The novice mistress trained us in everything, and this she did in great

AGNES'S FIRST EXPERIENCES IN INDIA

In a letter to the editors of Catholic Missions *and included in Lush Gjergji's biography,* Mother Teresa: Her Life, Her Works, *Agnes Bojaxhiu relates her first impressions of India.*

"On December 27 we reached Colombo. Mr. Scalon, a brother of one of our Sisters, was waiting for us on the dock. We went to the missionary college of St. Joseph, where, in a poor chapel, we gave thanks to the Lord. After that, we proceeded to his house. With amazement we observed the life that unfolded in the streets. Among the crowds we could immediately pick out the Europeans in their elegant clothes from the dark skinned natives with their variously colored apparel. Most of the locals went about half naked. Their skin and hair appeared shiny in the hot sunlight. One could easily see that deep poverty was the lot of most of these people. We felt especially sorry for those who ran on, pulling their little rickshaws, like horses, through the streets. We all resolved that we would never use such means of transportation. But then Mr. Scalon, who was accustomed to these ways, decided to bring us to his house in one of these conveyances. We were all in consternation, and the other Sisters too were amazed, but we had to accept. All we could do was to pray that the load would prove light enough for the human horses. When we got to the house we all felt much happier.

Over here, nature is really marvelous. The whole city seems like one big garden. Tall palm trees bearing abundant fruit, lift their branches proudly to the sky, and almost every house boasts of beautiful flowering plants. As we beheld all this we prayed that God might in his mercy make their souls even more beautiful than their flowers."

Upon her arrival in India, Agnes was struck by the profound poverty experienced by many of the people.

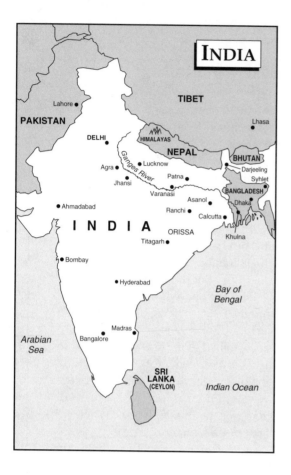

INDIA

Sister Teresa's duties involved more than teaching, however. That summer, before the fall term of school started, she began her service with a brief mission to a hospital in Bengal. A Jesuit priest working in the area, Janez Udovc, was impressed with Sister Teresa and her fellow sisters. He wrote to Zagreb about the new missionary sisters: "They are really happy and content. I am amazed at how well they look. They already speak English and Indian [Hindi] well, and now they are starting to learn Bengalese."[22]

Sister Teresa's duties included dispensing medicine to the poor who came to the hospital seeking treatment. The November 1931 issue of *Catholic Missions*, published in Zagreb, carried her letter describing the joy she felt in her work there:

> In the pharmacy of the hospital hangs a picture of the Redeemer surrounded by a crowd of sick people; you can read the tragedy of existence written on their faces. Every morning I look at this picture before I begin my work. This glance sums up all that I feel. Jesus, all for you and for souls! Next, I open the door. The little gallery is always crowded with sick, starving, unhappy people. All their eyes are fixed on me with indescribable hope. Mothers hand me their sick babies, just as the people in the picture do. My heart beats with joy; I can keep up your work, O Jesus. I can calm many sorrows; I console and heal, repeating the words of the best Friend of souls.[23]

detail. . . . For two hours a day, from nine to eleven in the morning, we taught little boys and girls in St. Teresa's School. It was a one-room school and there were generally about twenty boys and girls from the families who lived around us on the hillside.[21]

At the end of their two years, on May 24, 1931, Sister Teresa entered a six-year period of testing and preparation known as the profession of temporary vows. This period started with a ceremony during which she made her first promise (renewed annually) to practice poverty, chastity, and obedience to her religious superiors.

CLEANING UP AT ST. TERESA'S PRIMARY SCHOOL

In one of her early letters, Sister Teresa is quoted by Lush Gjergji in Mother Teresa: Her Life, Her Works. *Sister Teresa tells about the preparations she made for her first class in the slum parish school.*

"When they first saw me these little ones asked themselves if I were an evil spirit, or maybe a goddess. For them, everything is black or white. Whoever deals gently with them is adored like one of their divinities, whereas they are afraid of people who are harsh with them, as though they were demons, and they limit themselves to respecting them.

I rolled up my sleeves, moved everything out of the room, took water and a mop, and began to clean the floor. This surprised them a great deal. They stayed there watching me for a long time, because they had never seen a teacher start a lesson with similar work, especially since in India, cleaning is done by people of inferior classes. Seeing me happy and smiling the girls began to help me, while the boys brought more water. After two hours that untidy room was changed, at least to some extent, into a schoolroom, where everything was spick and span. It was a rather long room, which at one time had served as the chapel; today it is divided into five classrooms. . . .

When we got to know each other better they could not contain themselves for joy. They began dancing and singing around me until I had placed a hand on each of those dirty little heads. From that day on they called me 'Ma,' which means mother. How little it takes to make simple souls happy!"

But ministering to the health needs of the poor would not be her permanent assignment.

LORETO HOUSE IN CALCUTTA

Sister Teresa, the Loreto superiors had decided, was not to work in a hospital but instead on the campus of Loreto House as a teacher at St. Mary's School. The Loreto sisters strongly supported education and considered it the means through which the local people could work their way out of poverty. Biographer Eileen Egan describes the school as "situated in an extensive compound behind a solid wall, broken only by an impressive entrance erected in the classic style with two columns on each side. [And] generally referred to as Loreto Entally."[24]

Sister Teresa was assigned to teach two hundred Bengali girls geography, history, and catechism in their native language. Her fellow teachers were Bengali women of a relatively new congregation, the Daughters of St. Anne. This diocesan order, founded by Loreto in 1898, allowed the sisters to wear a blue sari, a simple garment that consists of several yards of cloth draped so that one end forms a skirt and the other end forms a head covering.

In line with the high educational goals of the Loreto sisters, Sister Teresa soon was herself taking more college classes. By 1935 she was preparing for advanced examinations.

After obtaining her degree, Sister Teresa was given the additional job of being in charge of St. Teresa's Primary School in a nearby parish. In 1936 and 1937 she walked several blocks to teach in this poor school, holding catechism classes at St. Mary's before she left and, after she came back at 4:00 P.M., supervising the children's recreation hour there.

LIFE VOWS IN LORETO

The six years of Sister Teresa's temporary profession in Calcutta went by quickly and happily. She now prepared for the day when her vows would commit her entire lifetime to the prayer and work of her religious community. Following the custom of the Sisters of Loreto, she would then advance from being called "Sister" to being called "Mother."

A modern Loreto sister waits for her students at the convent school. In keeping with Loreto's educational mission, Sister Teresa vowed to devote her life to teaching.

In the tradition of the founder of Loreto, the Englishwoman Mary Ward, whose ministry was "the Christian education of maidens and girls,"[25] she would devote her life to teaching. But she would no longer go outside the walls for her work, for she was now subject to strict enclosure rules.

The rule of enclosure may have been easier on her than it was on the children she had been teaching. In 1937 she wrote of this experience at St. Teresa's Primary School:

This happened a short time before I made my final vows. One day a little fellow came to me, pale and sad. He asked me if I would come back to see them, because he had heard that I was going to become "Mother." Then he started to cry and told me with tears: "Oh, don't become a Mother." I drew him close to me and asked him: "What is wrong, my boy? Don't be afraid. I will come back."[26]

On May 24, 1937, at her final vow ceremony in Darjeeling, Agnes Gonxha Bojaxhiu, now to be known as Mother Teresa, promised to follow the Loreto sisters' discipline for the rest of her life. Along with the other sisters, she would attend the community mass and spend time in prayer before breakfast. After a long school day, there would be more community prayer. It would be a life of self-denial, lack of privacy, and prescribed reading. She would wear a garment that looked like everyone else's and live a life without a husband or children of her own. For her it would be a happy life because, as she said later, "we do it for Jesus."[27]

A PROFESSED LORETO NUN AT ENTALLY

After final vows, Mother Teresa returned to Loreto Entally, where she continued teaching at St. Mary's. Although now subject to cloister rules, she was, nevertheless, aware of the world outside her walls. Under the direction of her mentor, Mother Mary of the Cenacle, she learned school administration and became headmistress of St. Mary's while still teaching her geography and history classes.

Strict as Mother Teresa's training was, she was allowed to keep in touch with her family by letter. She was now writing to Drana and Aga in Tiranë, Albania, where they been reunited with Lazar. Aga worked as a translator and radio broadcaster to support their mother, who had been persuaded to give up her business and her house in Skopje.

AGNES'S FAMILY

In 1934, Drana moved to Tiranë, Albania, where her son, Lazar, was a stableman in the service of the Albanian king. To biographer Lush Gjergji, author of Mother Teresa: Her Life, Her Works, *Lazar gave this account of how Drana moved from Skopje to Tiranë.*

"[In 1932] I wrote to my mother to take all the personal documents and the titles to our property and to come and live with me. She got together a few papers, a couple of fine carpets and some embroidery, and in 1934 she arrived at Tirana. When I saw her I ran up to her to embrace her. 'Are you Lazzaro?' she asked. 'Don't you recognize me?' I answered, and then we went home. For me it was the happiest of days, one I never forgot."

Because of her correspondence with them, Mother Teresa kept up the Albanian language. Spiritually, she had her sister's devotion and self-sacrifice and her mother's religious idealism to hold before her as she lived out her mission.

She wrote this letter to her mother about her work at St. Mary's:

> I am sorry not to be with you, but you can be pleased, dear mother, because your little Agnes is very happy. . . . I am living a new life. Our center is a lovely place. I teach, and this is the kind of work I like best. I am also in charge of the whole school, and everyone here loves me.[28]

Her mother wrote back:

> My dearest daughter, do not forget that you went out there to help the poor. Do you remember old Filja? She is covered with sores, but what bothers her the most is to realize that she is all alone in the world. We do what we can to help her; indeed, the worst thing is not the sores but the fact that she had been forgotten by her family.[29]

More Responsibility

Mother Teresa's duties continued to multiply. Her fluency in Hindi, Bengali, and English, reminiscent of her father's ability to speak many languages, surely contributed to the fact that she was put in charge of the Daughters of St. Anne. Also assigned to be moderator of the local chapter of the Sodality of the Blessed Virgin Mary, she guided the adolescent girls of St. Mary's in their first attempts at putting their faith to work, much as she had done as a young woman in Skopje.

Her students in the sodality indirectly kept her in touch with the nearby *bustee*, or slum, called Moti Jihl, which was located on the other side of the wall from St. Mary's. Father Julian Henry, the sodality's director and the Jesuit pastor of St. Teresa's, kept the St. Mary's girls busy working for the poor. Those involved in sodality service projects in the *bustee* visited families, helped the sick draw water from the nearby dirty pond, and worked at Nilratan Sarkar Hospital, also located nearby, visiting and running small errands for the patients.

The Outside World Encroaches

Outside Loreto Entally, World War II engulfed Mother Teresa's world. She soon found herself explaining the events of the war to her students. As a history and geography teacher, she had to explain how Great Britain's involvement in the war meant India's involvement as well. When Japanese troops invaded neighboring Burma, once even bombing Calcutta, she explained why their city, because of its location, was being overrun by refugees and beset with poverty.

As part of the history lessons, Mother Teresa taught of the campaigns of Mahatma Gandhi to improve the plight of the poor in India by nonviolent resistance to British rule of the nation. As the war drew to a close and the time for India's

THE LORETO GIRLS

Eileen Egan's biography, Such a Vision of the Street *includes this assessment of Loreto Entally, the school compound at Calcutta where Mother Teresa taught for nineteen years.*

"The Loreto Sisters, from the memorable day of their arrival [in Calcutta] on December 30, 1841, had made a deep impact on Bengali society through the education of women and girls. Besides their six high schools in Calcutta, they conducted at Loreto House a University College for Women. This was the first of their Loreto colleges, others being opened in Lucknow and Darjeeling for later generations of Indian women. From their first foundation in Calcutta, the women of Loreto moved out to initiate centers of education for women and girls across the subcontinent from Dacca to Delhi to Bombay. The young women who received degrees from Loreto College were referred to admiringly as 'Loreto Girls' and took responsible places in education and social welfare in the city, the province, and the nation. In free India, a Loreto graduate became the first woman judge of the Delhi High Court; another served as judge of the High Court of Calcutta. Others were elected to the Indian Parliament. . . .

As the life of religious Sisters is the very model of 'regularity and order,' no better guides could be found for the inculcation of these qualities. The various European Christian groups in Calcutta, many of them critical of the Catholic Church as a whole, recognized this, as did many Hindu, Parsi, and Anglo-Indian families. They entrusted their daughters to the 'Ladies of Loreto' in successive generations."

The Sisters of Loreto have been dedicated to the education of women and girls since 1841. Here, modern-day "Loreto Girls" cheer at a sporting event.

independence neared, the world outside Loreto Entally intruded even more.

When Loreto Entally was requisitioned by authorities as a military hospital, Mother Teresa facilitated the evacuation of Loreto boarding students. She met refugee missionaries from the Far East—Good Shepherd Sisters and Maryknoll Sisters. Continuing her duties as director for the Daughters of St. Anne from a makeshift center on Convent Road, she learned of their sorrows for relatives lost in the war.

Even the end of World War II failed to bring peace to India. As conflict between Muslims and Hindus intensified, Calcutta, with large populations of both faiths, was wracked with riots. Inside Loreto Entally, Mother Teresa found the opportunity to again practice *besa*. As she later said:

> We had been behind our safe walls. We knew that there had been rioting. People had been jumping over our walls, first a Hindu, then a Muslim.
>
> You see, our compound was between Moti Jihl, which was mainly Muslim then, and Tengtra, with the potteries and the tanneries. That was Hindu. We took in each one and helped him to escape safely.[30]

NEW INSPIRATION

The ongoing violence disrupted all deliveries of food to Loreto Entally. Mother Teresa later said that she did what she had to do:

> I went out from St. Mary's Entally. I had three hundred girls in the boarding school and we had nothing to eat.
>
> We were not supposed to go out into the streets, but I went anyway.
>
> Then I saw the bodies on the streets, stabbed, beaten, lying there in strange positions in their dried blood. . . .
>
> When I went out on the street—only then I saw the death that was following them.
>
> A lorry full of soldiers stopped me and told me I should not be out on the street. No one should be out, they said.
>
> I told them I had to come out and take the risk. I had three hundred students who had nothing to eat. The soldiers had rice and they drove me back to the school and unloaded bags of rice.[31]

The problem of food had been solved, but what she had seen left Mother Teresa with a much tougher dilemma. As she traveled that year to Darjeeling for her annual retreat, Mother Teresa thought about what she had seen and about her life in Loreto Entally. She became convinced that she had received another call from God. As she later reflected:

> I was going to Darjeeling to make my retreat. It was on that train that I heard the call to give up all and follow Him into the slums—to serve Him in the poorest of the poor. I knew it was His will and that I had to fol-

Dead bodies lie in the streets of Calcutta following bloody rioting in 1946. When riots disrupted food deliveries to the school, Mother Teresa risked her life by going out on the streets to find food for her students.

low Him. There was no doubt that it was to be His work.

I was to leave the convent [walls] and work with the poor while living among them. It was an order. I knew where I belonged, but I did not know how to get there.[32]

Mother Teresa completed her retreat. During that month, she wrote out her understanding of her new calling to leave the walls of Loreto Entally, to go beyond every wall that separated her from the life of the poor, and to take her vows of service to God into the street.

3 Testing a New Calling (1946–1960)

Mother Teresa's month-long retreat in the mountains near Darjeeling was an ideal time and place for her to work out her new calling. She was convinced that she should work freely in the world, with no rule of enclosure. In her retreat journal, she wrote in detail of what she envisioned as her new apostolate, which included relinquishing the traditional starched veil and habit in favor of a sari. Her plan of discarding the habit was not as revolutionary as might have been

In the mountains near Darjeeling, Mother Teresa pondered what she believed was her new calling—working and living among the poorest of the poor.

thought. Her work with the Daughters of St. Anne had taught her that native Bengali sisters were not required to wear a habit.

TESTING THE CALL FROM GOD

When Mother Teresa returned to Calcutta in the middle of October, she immediately began to work toward following her call. In her mind, it was impossible to just walk out of Loreto Entally as if she had not totally committed herself to the church. Her final vows meant that she had not only promised to obey God but also owed obedience to several church superiors. To go ahead without their permission would be to break her vow.

The first person to whom she went for advice was a Jesuit priest named Father Celeste Van Exem. He was her spiritual director; that is, a priest she trusted to guide her in the practical aspects of giving her life to God. Father Van Exem knew her very well, even to such details as the fact that she liked to move furniture and the fact that she was resting several hours a day because of recurrent respiratory problems. Van Exem was an experienced missionary in Calcutta, and he was in contact with a fellow Jesuit, Archbishop Ferdinand Perier, who would be the one to approve any new missionary work in the diocese.

The archbishop told Van Exem that Mother Teresa must wait a year, and she must not talk or write to anyone but her spiritual director about her hopes and dreams. She must do what her Loreto su-periors asked of her, remaining inside the enclosure. In the meantime, he would think about the feasibility of a European woman working in the streets of Calcutta dressed in a sari.

Mother Teresa set about the next task she was assigned. What her superiors asked was that she go from Calcutta to Asansol, three hours away by train, to work in the convent school there. For the whole year of 1947, while waiting for the archbishop's decision, the only person to whom she mentioned her plans was Van Exem.

ON HER WAY TO THE STREETS OF CALCUTTA

The year 1947 brought great political and economic upheaval. It became clear that India would soon be independent from Great Britain, a fearful certainty since conflicts between Muslims and Hindus remained unresolved. India received its independence on August 15, 1947. With sovereignty also came partition into two new countries: India and Pakistan. Violence soon followed, and bloody rioting filled the streets of Calcutta.

As 1947 drew to a close, the archbishop told Mother Teresa that she should write to the mother general of Loreto in Ireland about her desire. With the understanding that he would review her letter first, he promised that he would continue to work with her on her missionary plans.

This letter turned out to be a most grueling test of Mother Teresa's dedication to obedience. She wrote to Mother Gertrude

Violence and rioting erupted once again in the streets of Calcutta in 1947 after India gained its independence from Great Britain.

M. Kennedy in Ireland, asking to be released for one year from the enclosure (a permission formally known as exclaustration) for her work in the streets.

But the archbishop would not let Mother Teresa send this letter. He insisted that she ask to be released from her religious vows; she must, he insisted, use the word *secularization* instead of *exclaustration*. Once again, Mother Teresa complied with his directives, and the letter was sent to Ireland.

Mother Gertrude, in response, told Mother Teresa to write to the church authorities in Rome for exclaustration.

Once again the archbishop insisted on reviewing her letter and he insisted that she ask for secularization. Mother Teresa again wrote as he asked. The letter was sent to Rome in February 1948.

The response, which came in July, seemed like a miracle to Mother Teresa. The highest church authorities had granted her original request, exclaustra-

tion. Finally the archbishop had to agree that Mother Teresa could keep her vows while working in the streets.

ANOTHER YEAR OF TESTING THE CALL

Mother Teresa now was back to being called Sister Teresa, for the rule of enclosure and being called "Mother" went together. The day after she signed her exclaustration decree, she asked Father Van Exem to bless her chosen clothing for her new mission work—a white cotton sari trimmed with a blue stripe, a garment like that typically worn by widows in India.

To help her prepare for her new calling, Sister Teresa took two crucial steps. She applied for citizenship in India, and she wrote to the Medical Mission Sisters at Holy Family Hospital in Patna, in the state of Bihar, asking to take a short course in medical technology and nursing practices. Within a week she had her invitation in hand, bought a train ticket, and set out on her new journey. Sister Stephanie Ingendaa, who ran the hospital in Patna, tells how their relationship started:

> In August 1948 I received in Patna a letter from Sr. Teresa asking me whether it would be possible for her to stay with us at the hospital for a few months, live with the Indian Sisters who were in nurses' training and make contact with the people. She explained that she had received one

Rather than the traditional nun's starched veil and habit, Mother Teresa chose to wear a simple white cotton sari trimmed with a blue border.

year of exclaustration from Rome. She was going to work in future for the poor and destitute in Calcutta. Of course, I wrote her that she could come and stay as long as she would like. From that came my first known meeting with Mother Teresa, but we were often in contact after that.[33]

Training with the Medical Mission Sisters took place in a school building remodeled as a clinic. One of the doctors, Sister Elise Wynen, recalled that Sister Teresa did whatever she could to be helpful:

> We were much too busy to hold long discussions with Mother Teresa. She was just fitted into a cubicle, given a chair in the dining room and community room, and included into our day. Whenever there was a new admission, an emergency or an operation or delivery, Mother Teresa was called at the same time as the nurse called the doctor. She would come flying across the lawn and stay with the patient. She often needed help from the nurses for Hindi terms since she was more fluent in Bengali.[34]

BACK TO CALCUTTA

By the end of three months in Patna, Sister Teresa felt ready to deal with disease and death in Calcutta. She pinned a crucifix to her shoulder with a safety pin, accepted a gift of five rupees beyond the money for her train ticket, and at the beginning of December 1948, she returned to Calcutta, which was now swollen with

Mother Teresa greets school children in Calcutta, where her first project was the formation of a school for children of the city's slums.

thousands of newly arrived refugees both from the new country of Pakistan and from the northern agricultural regions where drought had destroyed thousands of acres of rice. Like many of the refugees she had come to help, she was a poor woman, homeless, and on the street.

Her spiritual director, Father Van Exem, talked to her about getting sufficient sleep, and she obtained a room at St. Joseph's Home, where the Little Sisters of the Poor cared for about two hundred destitute people. After a few days of helping there, she was more sure than ever that she must go into the street. She started walking about, looking for the work she believed God wanted her to do.

After an hour's walk from the home, she was back in the neighborhood of Loreto Entally. Everywhere there were children on the street. The obvious need, they seemed to be saying, was a school.

The pastor of St. Teresa's, Father Henry, remembered Sister Teresa and was glad to have her back in his neighborhood. He provided the names of some parents in his parish, and soon the first five students eagerly gathered around her.

HER MISSION TAKES SHAPE

In a short time, people learned that Sister Teresa had returned. Youngsters who remembered her, though, got a surprise when they saw her:

Used to seeing her in a nun's habit, they got a shock seeing her wearing a sari of the cheapest kind. In the Calcutta of 1948, she must have presented a strange sight indeed: a European, and yet not one. True, there were plenty of European women married to Indians, but they wore fine silk and cotton saris. Nor were their feet ever exposed: Mother Teresa's bare feet were encased in rough leather sandals, a parting gift from the Patna Sisters.[35]

To help him make his upcoming decision about her work, Archbishop Perier asked that Sister Teresa keep a written account of how she spent her days. Consequently, there exists a small book of notes about her days from December 25, 1948, to June 13, 1949.

In the beginning, according to her book, she asked for and received donations for her work. The pastor of the Park Circus parish gave her one hundred rupees, which she used to rent two school rooms. In her book, Sister Teresa writes: "I rented two new rooms for five rupees each per month, to use for the school and dispensary. It is right in front of a big [water] tank."[36]

By December 28 she had twenty-one children in her school and a volunteer from St. Mary's to help her. In her book she records, "Those who were not clean, I gave a good wash at the tank," and "I laughed a good many times as I had never taught little children before. The *kaw-khaw-gaw* (letters of the Bengali alphabet) did not go so well. We used the ground instead of a blackboard—everybody was delighted."[37]

Before the end of the month, Sister Teresa had two more projects going. She opened a dispensary in a room at the school to screen tuberculosis patients. She also started a second school on January 19 and had enrolled twenty-three children within two weeks.

TWIN PROBLEMS TO SOLVE: VOLUNTEER HELP AND HOUSING

To gain additional support for her three projects, Sister Teresa requested permission to place notices in church bulletins asking for volunteer workers and money. She had some response, but the volunteers were not always able to come.

For Father Van Exem, however, finding volunteers was not as urgent as finding somewhere nearby for Sister Teresa to live. As Van Exem explains, Father Henry, pastor of St. Teresa's parish, helped him find a place:

> Father Henry and I went about on our cycles to East Calcutta and other places, trying to find a suitable house. Then it struck me all of a sudden that Alfred and Michael Gomes, two brothers whom I knew, were living in a nice, three-storeyed house. I knew that the top floor was vacant. Mother [Teresa] could begin there, and then slowly things would improve.[38]

The suggestion worked out. At the end of February, Sister Teresa moved into an empty room at the top of a wooden staircase in the Gomes home, located at 14 Creek Lane, a mixed residential and business street.

TESTING THE WATERS AT ST. MARY'S

One of the early Missionaries of Charity, Sister Florence, was known as Agnes Vincent while she was a student in St. Mary's. In this interview with Desmond Doig, excerpted from Mother Teresa: Her People and Her Work, *she tells how Mother Teresa tried to inspire the girls at St. Mary's to help the very poorest people.*

"She was testing our minds, inspiring us, giving us encouragement. Always from the terrace of our school she could see the slums. I suppose we knew she'd be leaving. When the time came, we gave her a farewell. We sang something beautiful, in Bengali—they were farewell songs. The children gave her something and everybody was in tears. From the reception I think she went to the church and from there she left. We didn't see her any more. We heard she'd gone to Patna for medical training, and then that she was back and had started working amongst the poor. Soon she came fishing to our homes, talking to our parents and to us. We were sitting for our School Final exams then, so our parents thought study was more important than anything else. But Mother said, 'No, no, the sooner you come, the better.' She was young-looking and very dynamic. She inspired us. So we joined her, Sister Agnes first, then Sister Gertrude and Sister Dorothy. We went two and three at a time and formed a group. There were twelve of us without Mother, exactly like the Apostles. Then one left because she found it was not her vocation. Four of us carried on studying for our School Finals after joining Mother and she used to coach us to make sure we passed."

A SORT OF CONVENT

Physical housing met some of Sister Teresa's needs but not all. There were times when loneliness overcame her:

Today, my God, what tortures of loneliness. I wonder how long my heart will suffer this. Tears rolled and rolled. Everyone see my weakness. My God give me courage now to fight self and the tempter. Let me not draw back from the Sacrifice I have made of my free choice and conviction. Immaculate Heart of my Mother, have pity on Thy poor child. For love of Thee I want to live and die a Missionary of Charity.[39]

By the next day she came up with a way to solve all three of her problems: volunteers, living quarters, and loneli-

Mother Teresa invited Sister Agnes (pictured), one of her former students, to become one of the first members of her new religious order.

ness. She wrote to one of her former St. Mary's students, Subhasini Das. This young woman, who took the name Sister Agnes, later recalled:

One day [while I was at St. Mary's] I told Mother Teresa, "You have often spoken about the need to start this kind of work. We are ready to help, but we need a leader. Why can't you be our leader?" It just came out spontaneously. Mother smiled, but hushed me into silence. It was then that I first realized that something was already going on in her mind. When she fi-nally left Loreto, it did not come to me as a surprise. When she moved to Creek Lane, she sent me a note asking me to meet her. I remember clearly that it was on 1 March that I went to see her. She asked me if I were ready. I replied that I was waiting only for a date and time. Mother Teresa suggested 19 March, which was St. Joseph's feast day. I could hardly wait. On that day, I entered into my new life, which has brought me only happiness in serving God.[40]

Sister Teresa's spirits were buoyed on March 26 when a second of her former pupils, Magdalena Gomes (no relation to Alfred and Michael) joined them. From letters written at the time, in which she referred to Subhasini and Magdalena as postulants, and to their home as a convent, it is clear that a plan of starting a new religious order was crystallizing.

In keeping with the values of her youth and of her Loreto life, Sister Teresa had both of the young women finish their studies, Subhasini to be a teacher and Magdalena to be a nurse.

From these small beginnings, the slum ministry grew rapidly. Father Henry's parish started taking up a regular collection to pay for a feeding program for the poor. In addition, more former students of St. Mary's came to join the community until there were ten postulants; by the end of the summer, they had to ask their landlords for another room. All ten postulants wore the white sari and ordered their life like nuns. They rang bells signaling meal-times and prayers and kept a prayerful silence in their

THE FIRST MISSIONARIES OF CHARITY

Sister Bernard Rozario, one of the pioneers in Mother Teresa's fledgling congregation, tells Desmond Doig in Mother Teresa: Her People and Her Work *about the way they lived in their poor convent.*

"Now when we tell these other Sisters how we, in the first group, lived, they can't believe. They say it's incredible. It was. It must have been.

We had to wash our clothes every day because we were in contact with infectious diseases. We used the cheapest soap in the market. We used to think that washing-powder was for the rich. Remember, most of us were studying in College at the time. Our Order had not yet been started. Rome only gave permission in October 1950.

We were wearing the plainest white saris, like our novices do now. Mother was about thirty-five, thirty-six. She was very energetic. . . . She used to teach and train us at home and manage the work outside. She never showed us she needed extra help outside. She just told us, 'You are students. Go and study.' We gave her a helping hand of course, but she never felt helpless on her own. It was tough. And she wanted it to be tough. She didn't want to make it easy and she was not arbitrary with her ideals, her charismatic gift. She was moving around and doing things, so she didn't notice the hardship.

We had the cheapest food, poor food, but Mother made us eat plenty so we didn't have to depend on other expensive nourishing things. Mother was always afraid that we might get TB or things like that. But we kept good health.

Our first constitution was that no one could stay at home, not even to cook. So we used to take turns to cook a little in the morning and the rest when we came home. Now some stay at home for office work and to receive phone calls and guests and visitors. That is because the work has expanded so much."

small space. For their recreation, however, they played loud and vigorous ball games or tug-of-war outdoors.

Father Van Exem considered it part of his responsibility to ensure that the young women had enough to eat. He put an ad in the newspaper, which brought in a donation from the chief minister of Bengal, R. C. Roy. Sister Teresa also took seriously the need for sufficient food, even if she had to beg. When she went out in search of food, Sister Teresa could be extremely effective. Her landlords, Alfred and Michael Gomes, recalled how she returned from Howrah Station, the immense railway terminal across the Hugli River, after such a trip:

> She left early that morning, well before eight, and returned at about five in the evening. I was surprised to find that she was sitting in the back of a truck on top of some bags of flour and rice . . . to make sure that nothing was stolen and that her girls had something to eat.[41]

A STRONG FOUNDATION

At the end of her year of probation, Sister Teresa formally requested that the archbishop authorize a new congregation of sisters to be called the Missionaries of Charity. Archbishop Perier commissioned Father Van Exem and Sister Teresa to write a formal rule, spelling out exactly how the sisters would live and work, and to submit it to him before April 1, 1950, when he was scheduled for a visit to Rome. If the rule satisfied him, he promised, he would seek authorization to approve the Missionaries of Charity as a congregation for the diocese of Calcutta.

According to the document Sister Teresa and Father Van Exem submitted, the sisters would live in poverty, chastity, and obedience. In addition, by a fourth vow, they would promise "to give wholehearted and free service to the poorest of the poor."[42] They would live together in a convent but not according to the rule of enclosure.

In a remarkably short time, by October 7, 1950, the new congregation was approved by authorities in Rome. At a special mass celebrated by Archbishop Perier to mark the official beginning of the new congregation, one of the rooms in the Gomes home was consecrated as a chapel. From that day, the missionaries would have ten years to establish their ministry in Calcutta. After that, the mission could broaden if it was found to be successful.

Once again, Agnes Gonxha Bojaxhiu was to be known as Mother Teresa, this time as the founder of her own congregation. In a very real sense, she would be a mother: Not only must she direct the work of the missionaries and find food, she must also provide housing and training for a growing band of missionaries.

And more novices were coming. One was a Slavic Loreto sister, Mother Bernard Orzes, from Mother Teresa's own hometown of Skopje, who took the name Sister Francis Xavier. Within two years there were twenty-eight sisters. They were bursting the seams of Michael and Alfred Gomes's home.

A more appropriate building was found in February 1953 at 54A Lower Circular Road, and the archbishop loaned Mother Teresa enough money to buy it. As for finding work to do, that was never a problem; the missionaries saw more and more needs in Calcutta's crowded slums.

HOUSING FOR THE SISTERS

In Mother Teresa: The Authorized Biography, *Navin Chawla relates interviews he conducted with Sister Agnes (Subhasini Das) and Father Van Exem in which they told of the providential way in which the Missionaries of Charity received their new home.*

"One day, recalled Sister Agnes, a man arrived at Creek Lane with news that a suitable building was for sale. He offered to show Mother Teresa the property, located at 54A, Lower Circular road, and to take her to the vendor. When Mother Teresa met Dr. Islam, a magistrate, he was astonished that anyone should have known of his intention to sell, as he had discussed the matter only with his wife. Meanwhile, the man who had led Mother Teresa there had vanished. When Islam heard of their work, he was touched, recalled Sister Agnes. 'Money is not everything,' he said to Mother Teresa.

[Father Van Exem and the archbishop] went to see the place, [said Father Van Exem]. Islam stood in front of the house and just looked at it. He seemed to be very moved. After some time he asked me if he could step out for a while, as he wished to go to the nearby mosque of Maula Ali to pray. I said I would wait in the little room which was later to become the parlor. When he returned, he stood in front of the house again. There were tears in his eyes. He said, 'God gave me this house. I give it back to Him.' And then we parted. I never saw him again. He sold the house to the Archbishop, I don't think for very much."

THE MINISTRY BROADENS

The needs for the missionaries' services grew every day as political upheaval caused by the partition of Bengal into East Pakistan and the Indian state of West Bengal, along with drought in the countryside, brought thousands of refugees to Calcutta. Mother Teresa's response was simple and direct: If she walked around a corner and saw a person in need, she simply stopped right there and did what she could to help.

THE POOREST OF THE POOR

The needy the Missionaries of Charity saw were the dying, the children, and the lepers. The most clearly visible of Cal-

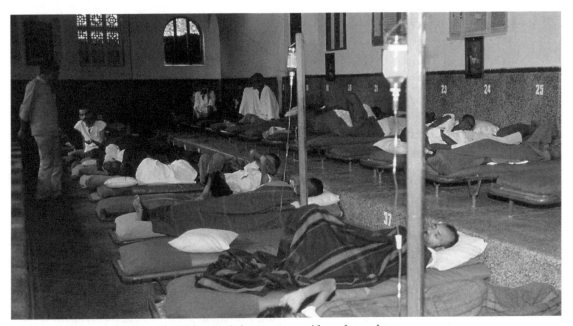

Mother Teresa opened Nirmal Hriday in Calcutta to provide a place where the dying poor could be cared for and allowed to die with dignity.

cutta's poor were the dozens who were dying in the street. These dying people were not accepted in the hospitals because they could not be cured. Mother Teresa's response was to find a place for them to die with dignity.

That place, she decided, was a rundown hostel located behind the Hindu temple of Kali along the banks of the Hugli River. On August 22, 1954, city officials gave Mother Teresa the use of the hostel if she would rehabilitate it. There, the missionaries gave the dying loving care—cleaning sores, bathing, offering a mat to lie on and a covering, touching them gently, and meeting their eyes and speaking to them of God's care, regardless of whether they were Muslim or Hindu, young or old, male or female, Indian or Pakistani. Although there were some ini-

tial protests among neighbors against locating the hospice in the area, eventually Nirmal Hriday (Home of the Pure Heart) in Kalighat was accepted and supported by officials, medical institutions, and philanthropists.

In addition to the dying, abandoned children abounded. In many cases, their parents had died or could neither support nor house them. The children ran about half naked, begging or scavenging bits of food to keep themselves alive. Some were just infants left in trash heaps; others were brought to the sisters by mothers desperate to give their children a chance at life, a place to live. These street children were even worse off than the children in Mother Teresa's slum schools had been. They needed immediate care just to keep them alive, or, in the worst cases, a few

THE FOUNDING OF NIRMAL HRIDAY AT KALIGHAT

In City of Joy, *Dominique Lapierre tells the story of Mother Teresa's founding of Nirmal Hriday.*

"It was in June 1952. The monsoon cataracts were beating down upon Calcutta with a noise that seemed to herald the destruction of the world. A white figure, stooping under the deluge, was skirting the walls of the Medical College Hospital. Suddenly she stumbled upon something stretched out on the ground. She stopped and discovered an old woman lying in the middle of a pool of water. The woman was hardly breathing. Her toes had been gnawed to the bone by rats. Mother Teresa scooped her into her arms and ran to the door of the hospital. She found the emergency entrance, went into a reception room, and deposited the dying woman on a stretcher. Instantly an attendant intervened.

'Take that woman away immediately!' he ordered. 'There's nothing we can do for her.'

Mother Teresa took the dying woman in her arms and set off again at a run. She knew another hospital, not far away. Suddenly, however, she heard a rattle. The body stiffened in her arms and she realized that it was too late.

Putting down her burden, she closed the poor creature's eyes and made the sign of the cross as she prayed beside her in the rain. 'In this city, even the dogs are treated better than human beings,' she sighed as she turned away.

The next day, she rushed to the municipal building and besieged its offices. The persistence of this European nun in a white cotton sari was a source of considerable astonishment. One of the mayor's deputies finally received her. 'It's a disgrace that people in this city are forced to die in the streets,' she declared. 'Give me a house where we can help the dying to appear before God in dignity and love.'

One week later the municipality placed at her disposal a former rest house for Hindu pilgrims, next to the great Kali temple."

A dying man is escorted by Mother Teresa and her fellow sisters to Nirmal Hriday.

Mother Teresa blesses children at her orphanage in Calcutta. Called Shishu Bhavan, the orphanage was created to take care of the ailing and undernourished street children who might die without immediate attention.

loving touches and a drop of milk before they died. In response to the needs of these children, Mother Teresa rented a house located near the motherhouse for use as an orphanage. The orphanage was called Shishu Bhavan.

Sister Bernard Rozario, a former student at Loreto Entally, recalls these early days when the Missionaries of Charity had so much to do and such limited resources:

We realized that there were a lot of undernourished children and poor dying people that the hospitals could do nothing for. How many can they take? And besides, medicine alone is not enough. We just used to try and bring them a little relief on the streets. When they died we used to inform the police. For five years we did that, then Mother [Teresa] realized we had to open a home.

We were always begging for medicines. Mother used to beg from various missions, from her friends, from anybody. Now at least she receives donations, at that time she was unknown. She was almost on the street herself.[43]

THE LEPER MINISTRY

Some needs proved far harder to address. In 1955 the World Health Organization and the Indian government became interested in controlling leprosy. At the time at least 200,000 lepers lived just in Calcutta

In 1955, approximately 3 million people suffered from leprosy in India. Mother Teresa began operating her first mobile leprosy clinic in 1957 in order to minister to the lepers, who many refused to treat.

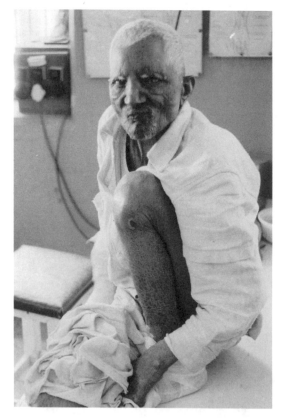

alone, a fraction of the 3 million lepers in India. Mother Teresa's first impulse was to establish a clinic for them where they could come to receive the newly developed drug dapsone. But ancient fears of the disease caused neighbors near the proposed site, which was located along the railroad tracks, to oppose the plan, and she was forced to abandon the clinic project.

Mother Teresa refused to abandon the lepers, however. When some Americans donated an ambulance, she converted it into a mobile treatment unit. With the help of Dr. P. C. Sen, a skin and leprosy specialist who was retiring from the Carmichael Hospital for Tropical Diseases, her first mobile leprosy clinic began operating in 1957.

THREE KEY WOMEN

Three women who helped Mother Teresa in those early days became important in bringing direct help to the poor. The first of these was Jacqueline deDecker, a Belgian woman who wanted to be a medical missionary in India. The second woman who proved to be of great help in Mother Teresa's expanding ministry was Ann Blaikie. This Englishwoman was living in Calcutta with her husband, Joseph, when Mother Teresa first went into the streets. The third key woman, American Eileen Egan, met Mother Teresa in 1955 when she was directing a food program to help refugees. These women's distinct roles in the life of Mother Teresa brought a variety of talents and connections to her program.

Running a new order that combined a belief in strict poverty with a mission of feeding and caring for the poor—which cost money—demanded diverse talents, and in deDecker, Blaikie, and Egan, Mother Teresa found the talents she needed.

Moreover, in that first decade after World War II, it was important to Mother Teresa to have some outlet for her feelings and aspirations at a time of isolation from all but one of the sisters she had known in Loreto, where she had spent nearly twenty years. Adding to Mother Teresa's isolation, the letters she had been accustomed to receiving from her mother and sister had been cut off by the Marxist regime that had taken over Albania, and she lost contact with her brother, Lazar, as well. So, from the beginning, these three women, each in her own way, were able to help guide and shape the new congregation.

JACQUELINE DEDECKER AND THE LINK WITH THE SUFFERING

Early on, while Sister Teresa was learning about medical procedures at the hospital in Patna, Jacqueline deDecker had sought her out. DeDecker had been trying to begin a ministry to the poor in Madras, in southern India. A friend had suggested that deDecker go to Patna to meet Sister Teresa. The two women became friends immediately, sharing their prayers and hopes. Their plan for deDecker to join the Missionaries of Charity never came to fruition, however, as deDecker's health required her to return to Belgium, where she was diagnosed with a spinal disease that would, even after many surgeries, cause almost complete paralysis. Realizing that deDecker could never become a Missionary of Charity, Mother Teresa continued to encourage her to give her life to God. On October 20, 1952, Mother Teresa extended an invitation to deDecker:

> Why not become spiritually bound to our Society, which you love so dearly? While we work in the slums etc., you share in the merit, the prayers and the work, with your suffering and prayers. The work here is tremendous and I need workers, it is true, but I need souls like yours to pray and suffer for the work. Would you like to become my spiritual sister and become a Missionary of Charity, in Belgium in body, but in soul in India?[44]

As partners in suffering and "twin spirits,"[45] as Egan describes them, Mother Teresa and deDecker founded a new branch of the missionaries called the Links for Sick and Suffering Co-Workers. Through this society, deDecker passed on to others the invitation expressed in Mother Teresa's letter of January 13, 1953: "I want specially the paralysed, the crippled, the incurable to join. In our turn, the Sisters will each one have a Sister who prays, suffers, thinks, writes to her and so is a second self."[46] A sick person who contacted deDecker from anywhere in the world was carefully paired with a Missionary of Charity and became a praying partner with the sister.

A letter from Mother Teresa explains her plan for the Links for Sick and Suffering Co-Workers to Jacqueline deDecker. It is quoted by Kathryn Spink in Mother Teresa: A Complete Authorized Biography.

"There will be no vows unless some get permission from their confessor to do so. We could get a few prayers we say, for you to say them also, so as to increase the family spirit, but one thing we must have in common—the spirit of our Society. Total surrender to God, loving trust and perfect cheerfulness—by this you will be known as a Missionary of Charity. Everyone and anyone who wishes to become a Missionary of Charity—a carrier of God's love—is welcome. . . . You see, my dear Sister, our work is a most difficult one. If you are with us—praying and suffering for us and the work—we shall be able to do great things for love of him—because of you."

ANN BLAIKIE AND THE CO-WORKERS OF MOTHER TERESA

Mother Teresa's second ally, Ann Blaikie, helped her make room for another kind of missionary, one who could contribute time and talents to the missions but who could not live the life of a sister. Blaikie joined the ministry of the Missionaries of Charity by choice, she says,

when I was heavily pregnant. . . . I had been working with others in a shop called "The Good Companions" in Calcutta, selling handiwork in aid of the missions until I became too pregnant and had to hand in my notice. One afternoon I was sitting on the balcony in the heat, wondering what on earth I could do and suddenly it just came to me—I would find Mother Teresa. I had never met her but I had read the occasional notice in the newspaper and I knew that a friend of mine had a vague connection with her.[47]

Shortly afterward, on July 26, 1954, Mother Teresa invited Blaikie to visit the little clinic she had started in Moti Jihl. They went on to Kalighat, discussing the needs of the children. Together the two women founded the group known as the Co-Workers of Mother Teresa. The group grew rapidly, and after just fifteen years the Co-Workers of Mother Teresa numbered in the thousands and were organized in most of the countries of the world.

EILEEN EGAN AND WORLDWIDE PUBLICITY

Mother Teresa was first approached by Eileen Egan, inspector of Catholic Relief Services (CRS) in India, in 1955. As the director in charge of the American Food for Peace program, she was of immense importance in continuing the feeding centers the missionaries had begun.

Almost immediately, Egan's position with CRS brought her into contact with Mother Teresa's other work. The hospital at Kalighat, the orphanage Shishu Bhavan, and the leper mobile units all made a deep impression on her.

As a sympathetic writer with international connections, Egan became a sort of informal public relations agent for the Missionaries of Charity. The books and articles Egan wrote brought Mother Teresa worldwide attention.

As part of her duties with CRS, Egan often accompanied Mother Teresa on her visits to prospective missions. Other than Mother Teresa herself, probably no one knew better than Egan the vast extent of Mother Teresa's work, even in its early years. Egan's contact and friendship would be a significant part of Mother Teresa's life to the very end.

By the time the Missionaries of Charity reached their tenth anniversary, the number of Mother Teresa's sisters had expanded to 119. The tiny school at Moti Jihl had grown to one in which 260 children were grouped into six classes. Fourteen other schools were also being run by the Missionaries of Charity. And from other dioceses in India, especially those from which young women had come to join the Missionaries of Charity, came many new calls for help.

As Mother Teresa saw it, the growth in her ministry and the network of local and international helpers were God's work. Far from being planned, each work was started as Mother Teresa saw the need. The need and the means to meet it arose simultaneously.

With the passing of the order's first decade, it was time for decisions regarding the missionaries' work. Church authorities were paying attention to Mother Teresa's efforts. August 1960 brought the case of the Missionaries of Charity once again to the attention of the papal nuncio, Archbishop James Robert Knox in Delhi, and to Pope John XXIII in Rome. They unhesitatingly approved Mother Teresa's desire to expand her mission beyond Calcutta.

Chapter

4 Expanding the Ministry to the Unwanted (1960–1970)

Immediately upon approval in 1960, Mother Teresa tested her sisters' ability to transcend Calcutta's culture. She sent sisters about two hundred miles southeast to Ranchi, a large city in what was known as the Tribal Belt. Easily reached by train, it had slums for the same reasons that Calcutta did—rural people were driven to urban centers by drought and crop failure.

Jhansi, located several hundred miles northwest of Calcutta on the Ganges River, was the next city to be opened to ministry. Situated near Delhi, the capital of India, the mission in Jhansi came to the attention of Prime Minister Jawaharlal Nehru; when the mission was ready, Nehru presided over the opening.

Success in her first two remote missions confirmed for Mother Teresa that a love of God and complete poverty were all the sisters needed. In her view, it was enough to have three saris each and a bucket in which to launder them. The very fact that they had left their homes and families to join the ministry, Mother Teresa believed, would convince God to send them whatever else they might need.

To bolster Mother Teresa's belief in the power of God to provide what she needed, there were experiences such as this one that she recounted to biographer Roger Marchand:

> [A] priest came up to me. He asked me to give a contribution to the press. I had left the house with five rupees, and I had given four of them to the poor. I hesitated, then gave the priest the one I had left. That afternoon, the same priest came to see me and brought an envelope. He told me that a man had given him the envelope because he had heard about my projects and wanted to help me. There were fifty rupees in the envelope. I had the feeling at that moment that God had begun to bless the work and would never abandon me.[48]

LEPERS, THE VERY POOREST OF INDIA'S POOR

Experiences like receiving the envelope with fifty rupees became common as local people responded to the work of the Missionaries of Charity. Mother Teresa's and her sisters' efforts were compatible with the Hindu belief in treating the poor with

THE FIRST LEPERS HELPED BY THE MISSIONARIES OF CHARITY

Malcolm Muggeridge, author and director of the video Something Beautiful for God, *spoke with Mother Teresa at some length. During this conversation, Mother Teresa told how their first leper patients came and how society treated the Indian lepers.*

"In 1957 we started with five lepers who came to our home because they had been thrown out from their work. They could get no shelter, they had to go begging. With them a doctor soon came to help us and he's still with us, Dr. Sen. He has also been training our Sisters for the leprosy work, because he's a specialist in leprosy work. Among the lepers there are many well-educated people, many rich and capable people. But owing to the disease, they have been thrown out of society, out of their homes, by their relations, and very often even their own children do not want to see them any more. They get isolated from their own families and have no alternative but to turn to begging. Very often you see people coming up to Bengal from the south and the Bengal people going to the furthest north just to be far away from the people and from the places where they have been known and served and loved. We have among our lepers here in Calcutta very capable people who have had very high positions in life. But owing to the disease, they are now living in the slums, unknown, unloved and uncared for. Thank God our Sisters are there to love them and to be their friends and to bring the rich closer to them."

love and compassion. The missionaries soon learned that the Hindu devotion to relieving pain and poverty flows from belief in the law of *karma*, which teaches that doing good deeds makes one worthy of reincarnation on ever higher levels of existence.

Mother Teresa came to understand that for Hindus, the suffering has yet another side to it. Marchand, in *Mother Teresa of Calcutta*: *Her Life and Her Work*, explains:

If they are in the lowest social caste, called *pariahs*, or untouchables, their condition is subhuman, [but] pariahs do not fight their condition; they believe they deserve it. To rebel would make them even less worthy, delaying their liberation from the wheel of

Lepers like this woman were very grateful for the help and compassion they received from Mother Teresa and her sisters.

surance of good *karma*. Their peace in suffering and their gratitude, it seemed to Mother Teresa, made the leper ministry pleasing to God.

FUNDING FOR LEPER VILLAGES

The ministry to India's leprosy victims grew. In the late 1950s and early 1960s, more and more of Mother Teresa's mobile units were making scheduled stops near the clusters of shacks where lepers lived. Funding for this leper ministry was always needed. In addition, Mother Teresa kept looking for better ways to help.

In 1961 a gift from the West Bengal government of thirty-four acres of completely undeveloped land in the coal-mining area of Asansol gave her a new idea. She thought of building a self-supporting village for people afflicted with leprosy. She knew that development of a village on the land, about a four-hour train ride north of Calcutta, could not be done without money. A place for leper families to live and work together in dignity would have to await the "miracle" of funding.

Before long, a powerful source began to offer some of the needed help. Almost immediately after Prime Minister Nehru had opened the Jhansi center of the Missionaries of Charity, he gave recognition to Mother Teresa's impact on India by nominating her for the Magnificent Lotus Award (the Padmashree). This high honor, announced annually on India's Republic Day and traditionally given only to Indians, was awarded to Mother Teresa on January 26, 1962.

rebirth. Pariahs are steeped in a centuries-old fatalism, and they are not hostile toward those more fortunate. . .

There are pariahs who literally are untouchable. In India lepers abound, living on the outskirts of cities and foraging for food scraps in garbage dumps. The poorest of India's poor, lepers are the favorites of Mother Teresa and her Sisters.[49]

Because the untouchables afficted with leprosy believed that they did not deserve relief from their condition, they were particularly grateful when they received help, and they gladly bestowed upon the giver the blessing they could give, an as-

Along with the award came fifty thousand rupees. With this sum Mother Teresa began to realize her dream of founding villages for lepers. While she used the award money to start her first stable leper village, in the northwestern city of Agra, she did not forget the Asansol land. It would still be available when the time was right.

ANOTHER MIRACLE AWARD

More than just the leper ministry came to benefit from funding "miracles." That same year Mother Teresa received the Magsaysay Award. The award came at a "miraculous" time for another project. She later recalled,

> A sister had telephoned from Agra to say they were desperately in need of a children's home . . . which would cost 50,000 rupees. . . . I told her it was impossible. Then the telephone rang again. This time it was from a newspaper, saying I'd been given the Magsaysay Award from the Philippines. I asked, "How much is it?" The man replied, "About fifty thousand rupees, Mother." So I called the Sister back to tell her God must want a children's home in Agra.[50]

FROM LIMOUSINE TO LEPER HOSPITAL

Meanwhile, the fact that Father Van Exem was now a parish priest in Asansol gave Mother Teresa motivation to visit there

Pope Paul VI was so impressed by the work he saw being done by the Missionaries of Charity in Bombay that he gave Mother Teresa his limousine, which she raffled off to raise money for a leper hospital.

from time to time and to keep in mind the thirty-four-acre plot of land nearby. Not until 1964, however, did the "miracle" of funds make possible a leper village on that site: when Pope Paul VI visited Bombay, American Catholics gave him a Lincoln Continental limousine to help him get about the city. Their gift became the "ticket" for the Asansol venture.

During his visit, Pope Paul had an opportunity to see what the Missionaries of Charity were doing. Impressed by their work, he gave the limousine to Mother Teresa. Ever practical, she held a raffle, and the sale of the raffle tickets earned the money needed to develop a hospital for the projected village.

TITAGARH ACCORDING TO SISTER BERNARD

Sister Bernard Rozario, one of Mother Teresa's original twelve sisters, gave Desmond Doig some details of the leper ministry for his biography Mother Teresa: Her People and Her Work. *Here, Sister Bernard summarizes the difficulties of serving some of the five thousand patients who are registered at the outdoor clinic at Titagarh.*

"They don't continue the treatment we give them. They leave long gaps during which time the disease worsens. You see, it's a long treatment and always there is the sad fact that poor lepers have nowhere to live. Their own people don't accept them. O yes, there are rich lepers. We have people like students from university and from very well-to-do homes and well-known families who come to take medicine. We had a girl about to get married who came here quietly to be cured. Her family had found that she had a leprous patch and they knew that if her in-laws-to-be discovered it, they would never allow the marriage. Fortunately, she was cured.

Then recently we had a little boy, about twelve, who told us that one day, while studying, he found his fingers getting stiff and crooked. There was no patch on him but he was a leper all the same. It's a nerve disease and once the nerves are affected they cripple and it is difficult to do anything at that stage. The disease can be arrested; restoring the nerves is almost impossible. That's how the terrible scars and ulceration come about. Lepers can't feel heat or pain in their extremities so they are often badly burned and maimed. Then the decay sets in. Age is no barrier; anyone can have it. We have found little children who are highly positive cases. We have had a six-month old baby with a leprous patch.

When you come to know leprosy patients, they are so nice. So great. And we learn much from them. You know what they say sometimes? 'We have leprosy outside, physically, but not on our hearts.' And they're very affectionate because we come into such close contact with them."

The importance of this permanent facility can hardly be exaggerated. Persons infected with leprosy but diagnosed soon enough can be cured; because its location could be publicized, the lepers' village could be a key factor in the early detection of the disease for those who otherwise might have allowed their illness to progress beyond its curable stages.

Thirty or so dwellings were soon being constructed on the Asansol site, and a chapel called Shantinagar (Place of Peace) soon became the center of life in the village. Mother Teresa turned over the direction of the village to her countrywoman, Sister Francis Xavier, who had by this time received a degree in medicine. The sister saw to it that the village around Shantinagar was, from its beginning, a model of beauty and sanitary conditions.

The "Miracle" at Howrah Station

No matter how much money was raised or how many volunteers arrived, the number of people to be served seemed to grow. The immense Howrah railroad station, across the Hugli River from Calcutta, provided a never-ending stream of new immigrants from East Pakistan and the north of India. The station was one of the places where the sisters went every day. As they tended the diseased and the dying, predominantly men who had fled drought and come to Calcutta hoping to support their families back home, Mother Teresa came to see the need for men and women both to participate in the ministry.

She spoke with various priests about starting a new men's order like her own, but neither of her old friends and helpers—Father Van Exem or Father Henry—felt he could be a cofounder. This presented a problem for Mother Teresa,

since it was simply unheard-of in the Catholic Church for a woman to start a men's order. Mother Teresa persisted, however, and on March 25, 1963, the Archbishop gave permission for her to begin the Missionary Brothers of Charity. "If not for her [Albanian] stubbornness, " biographer José Luis Gonzales-Baldado claims, "Mother Teresa might have given up her efforts to establish a male congregation, but her tenacity had its rewards."[51]

A Leader for the Missionary Brothers

Like the original Missionaries of Charity, the Missionary Brothers started small, with nine young men. For two years, under Mother Teresa's supervision, they went to Howrah Station to work with the men and boys. The brothers began simply, handing out bars of soap, then organizing evening meals and arranging vocational training for new arrivals.

Despite the initial success of getting the Missionary Brothers started, Mother Teresa still needed a director for them. Fulfillment of this need came in the form of an Australian named Ian Travers-Ball, who was in Bihar preparing to take his final vows as a Jesuit priest. As part of his required pastoral project, the Jesuits had sent him to Titagarh, site of Mother Teresa's first leper ministry.

After this introduction to life in the streets, Father Travers-Ball, following Mother Teresa's example, decided to ask for exclaustration from the Jesuits. In July 1966 he left the Jesuit order, just as Mother Teresa had left the Loreto order, and took

INDEPENDENCE FOR LEPERS

A Simple Path, compiled by Lucinda Vardey, includes Mother Teresa's perspective on the leper ministry now established where neighbors once refused to allow a clinic to be built.

"More than forty years ago we decided to start a mobile clinic for leprosy patients under a tree at Titagarh, several kilometers outside Calcutta. We saw patients twice a week and on the other days took care of those suffering from malnutrition and visited the homes of the sick. Then, on Saturdays, we'd do their cleaning.

Today, we have a wonderful center called Gandhiji Prem Nivas, which is almost a village in itself. Spread alongside the railway line, the buildings are painted in bright, cheerful colors: reds and blues and greens. There are workshops, dormitories, clinics, wards, a school, an outpatients' department, and also individual huts for families—as well as pools that provide the whole community with its water. Just inside the inner courtyard is a statue of Gandhi.

Prem Nivas was built by the leprosy patients themselves and is a place where they can both live and work. We first were given the land to develop in 1974, it was a railway dump yard. We began by building simple thatched huts and slowly it turned into something quite beautiful."

Mother Teresa's memoir is followed by words of Brother Viniod, who was running Gandhiji Prem Nivas at one time after the Missionary Brothers of Charity took over Titagarh:

"We have 1,400 leprosy cases under regular treatment per month and 38,000 have registered here since 1958. Many of them have been released from treatment; but those people we are now looking after are going to live for another twenty to thirty years, so that Missionaries of Charity will at least continue this work for that length of time. Now that leprosy can be controlled I am sure we will not see as much deformity in the future—the government's plan is to eradicate leprosy in India by the year 2000."

vows as Brother Andrew, head of the Missionary Brothers. The Titagarh leper mission was handed over to the Missionary Brothers and was renamed Gandhiji Prem Nivas. With a leader of their own, the brothers were given papal approval of their mission. In five years their numbers increased to ninety-two.

RENEWED CONTACTS
WITH FAMILY

With all of the organizations that Mother Teresa was starting and running, it is easy to understand that she had little time for personal interests. Though her mother and siblings had once more found a way to correspond outside of Albania, it was difficult for Mother Teresa to keep in touch. Aga's letters to Lazar would contain comments that referred to the infrequency of her communication:

> From Agnes I have not heard for a long time. Of course she has much to do and little time to spend with me. I am grateful to her because she promised to come and visit me when I can visit you. I am glad she is well. Today I will write to her too. A big hug, and lots of kisses. Your sister, Aga.[52]

In 1960 Mother Teresa had been sought out by her brother, Lazar, who had been exiled from Albania and was living in Rome with his wife, Maria. With the help of Eileen Egan and an Albanian priest, Lush Gjergji, Mother Teresa had even visited Lazar and Maria and their daughter and son-in-law, Aggi and Joseph.

Gjergji recalled how they had spoken about Drana and Aga, who were still living in Albania, and how they had begun to hope, as Lazar said,

> to do something to see once again their mother and sister. . . . [Lazar] told her, as he said to me, "Dear Agnes, don't lose hope; now we have many friends all over the world. I hope I will be able to do something for them."[53]

As years passed, Mother Teresa hoped that she might once again see her family. But by 1963, with the ten-year probation of her order only two years from completion, she had much to do in anticipation of this milestone. Family and homeland took a backseat to the preparation for the next steps in her order's ministry.

A CONGREGATION
ANSWERABLE TO THE POPE

Ministry to the poorest of the poor, the dying and diseased untouchables, was a day-to-day challenge for all who joined Mother Teresa's crusade. For dozens of young women to learn how to maintain joy and cheerfulness in the face of overwhelming misery, for them to learn Mother Teresa's spirit of prayer, required her to maintain personal contact with each of them. Showing her sisters how to love was Mother Teresa's means of proving God's love.

"Despite difficulties, dangers and personal hardships," writes Kathryn Spink, "Mother Teresa and many with her have been able to recognize in every act of human love . . . the 'proof' of an eternal love."[54] Maintaining the love they had been shown and taught was the ultimate test for many.

In the miracle of continuing vocations, dozens of young women passed this test, remaining faithful as they underwent the grueling experiences of cleaning stinking wounds, bathing emaciated bodies, feeding starving babies, and sharing the anguish of mothers whose children were dying.

By 1965, when the missionaries' ten-year probation had been completed, over three hundred women had come to the motherhouse on Lower Circular Road to join the Missionaries of Charity. This was a large enough number for the missionaries to be approved as a papal congregation. That meant that instead of answering to the bishop of Calcutta, they were now an international order and were directly responsible to the pope. They had certain requirements to fulfill, such as electing a mother general and other officers in a meeting called a general chapter. The Missionaries of Charity met for their first general chapter as a papal congregation in 1967, and they elected Mother Teresa as their mother general, to serve a term of six years. She still preferred not to be called "Reverend Mother," though. To her followers she would be just plain "Mother Teresa."

BEYOND INDIA

More important, from Mother Teresa's perspective, than her order's formal recognition by the pope, the congregation could now open missions outside of their own country. As it happened, the Missionaries of Charity was approved during the time the pope had convened a meeting of bishops from around the world, known as the Second Vatican Council. Among these influential church leaders, conversations soon resulted in word-of-mouth publicity for Mother Teresa's work, which in turn led to calls to expand her mission.

The first of the overseas calls came from Bishop Benitez of Barquisimeto, Venezuela. He wanted Mother Teresa to help the landless people of African descent who lived in the copper-mining region of Cocorote.

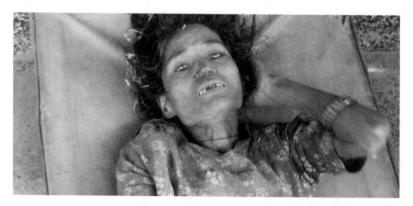

Maintaining a positive attitude was a constant challenge for Mother Teresa's sisters, who witnessed so much misery in their ministry, like that seen in the face of this dying woman at Nirmal Hriday.

This call was soon followed by calls from other places: Ceylon (1967), Tanzania and Rome (1968), Australia and Jordan (1969). In addition, by 1969, besides the Calcutta ministries, twenty-five missions were established in other dioceses around India.

THE MISSION IN SOUTH AMERICA

With the establishment of the South American mission, Mother Teresa's reputation for an inexhaustible endurance for worldwide travel began to grow. It was one of her inviolable rules that she must personally see every place to which she would send her sisters, and so Mother Teresa went to each country and area to assure herself that the sisters would be helping those truly in need and yet that they would be safe. She also required assurances that her sisters would have access to a priest so that they could go to mass on a daily basis.

The challenges the Missionaries of Charity faced were unique in each country they entered. As soon as the first missionaries arrived in Venezuela, they found that a comfortable home had been set up in anticipation of their coming. After giving away all but the simplest furnishings, the sisters turned their parlor into a vocational school, giving sewing and typing classes. They offered classes in English and themselves took classes in Spanish. Because the poor were often to be found in isolated rural areas, the sisters learned to drive a station wagon so they could visit the villages in the countryside.

Mother Teresa traveled frequently because she personally visited each new country and area where she intended to send her sisters.

IN ROME

Opportunities to help arose in unlikely places. In Rome, for example, twenty-two congregations were already working for the city's poor, so it was not anticipated that Mother Teresa's order would be asked to add a mission. However, in 1968, at the invitation of Pope Paul VI, she and three sisters flew to Rome to explore the possibility of establishing a mission there.

The day after they arrived, Mother Teresa found a small house among the city's poor. Mother Teresa was delighted to note that it was probably the poorest house

A NOVITIATE FOR ENGLISH CANDIDATES

In 1971, like the Loreto sisters, Mother Teresa decided to have a novitiate outside of India. Ann Blaikie, interviewed by Courtney Tower in "Mother Teresa's Miracle of Grace," related this story of how Mother Teresa found a house she thought to be suitable for a novitiate. But the house, in Southall, west of London, was for sale for nine thousand pounds.

"When the owner learned of Mother Teresa's purpose, she lowered her price. This still left us a huge problem—raising the 6000 pounds.

Then, . . . Mother Teresa visited Co-Workers around the country and carried, as usual, her old knitting bag with wooden handles. On her return, she handed the bag to [my] husband. 'I think there is some money in my bag,' she said. During her travels, people had, unsolicited, slipped money into it.

John Blaikie counted up handfuls of notes, checks, and coins. When he finished, he took a single 5-pound note from his pocket and added it to the collection. Looking at Mother Teresa, he said, 'This is the 6000 pounds to buy your house.'"

the Missionaries of Charity had yet occupied. The missionaries moved into the slum area and began their work among the poor coming in from Sicily and Sardinia.

AROUND THE WORLD, TO HER HOMETOWN, AND BACK TO CALCUTTA

As the 1960s drew to a close, the Missionaries of Charity continued to expand. In 1968 Tabora, Tanzania, became the order's first mission in Africa, followed by the first mission in Australia at Bourke. In 1970 the missionaries responded to a call to Melbourne, Australia, to work with drug addicts, alcoholics, prisoners, and juvenile delinquents, and then to a second Venezuelan mission.

In sad contrast, however, the country where Mother Teresa's sister and mother were living, Albania, continued to be almost impossible to enter. Although the Red Cross arranged for her to stop briefly in Prizren, in neighboring Yugoslavia, in 1970, it was another ten years before even Co-Workers of Mother Teresa were allowed to operate within that country. However, while she was in Yugoslavia, she had a long-time acquaintance, Monsignor Dorcic, take her to Skopje and to the shrine of the Madonna of Letnice.

After that, with the help of Eileen Egan she visited the Albanian embassy in Rome, trying more persistently to obtain permission to visit her sister and mother. Her pleas were to no avail. The Albanian officials either ignored her petitions altogether or refused to assure her that she could leave Albania if she once crossed into the country. Regretfully, she decided against risking a no-return trip into Albania, where she would be helpless to do anything connected with religion. Once more she turned from her family to the work of her missions, which was as urgent as ever. It must have seemed, at times, that no matter where she looked, the sick and needy were awaiting her touch. War, disease, and famine were everywhere. In fact, a series of even greater disasters was waiting for her at home in Calcutta.

5 Boundary Crossings (1970–1979)

Mother Teresa must have realized that the fate of poor and starving people in Calcutta was closely linked with the fate of those who lived in India's countryside. During the monsoon season, the numberless islands in the Ganges Delta, located just a few feet above sea level, were populated with two hundred thousand farmers living in temporary mud shelters while every available scrap of land was cultivated to provide food and cash crops for the rest of the year.

On November 12, 1970, the worst disaster of the century struck the struggling eastern province of Pakistan. A tropical storm blew across the Bay of Bengal, raising a tidal wave that destroyed six hundred thousand tons of crops, five hundred thousand houses, and from two hundred thousand to five hundred thousand human lives, not to mention bridges, the entire fleet of fishing boats, roads, and all means of communication. Mother Teresa's slum centers were flooded with refugees who surged across the border. Overburdened relief agencies rallied to help. Less than a year later another tropical storm and tidal wave on November 1, 1971, left ten thousand dead in India's eastern state of Orissa. Calcutta streets were once again filled with displaced persons.

Then, within just a few weeks, long-simmering disputes between India and Pakistan erupted into war. Refugees fled conflict in East Pakistan, streaming across the Howrah Bridge into Calcutta. Although an uneasy peace was soon restored, the peace agreement that resulted in the establishment of the independent nation of Bangladesh did not stop India's economy from being devastated by 10 million poor, diseased, and unemployed people pouring into the country. For Mother Teresa, the demands of hospitality exceeded anything she knew of Albanian *besa*.

The sisters, their feeding centers already in place, were immediately recognized as a valuable international asset. They cooperated with Indian government agencies, the United Nations, and Catholic Relief Services in efforts to help refugees. Within a month of the close of the war, Mother Teresa was across the border to the east, establishing centers in the new nation's areas of worst disaster—the capital city of Dhaka on January 21, 1972, and Khulna on February 11.

East Pakistanis flee the violence of the 1971 civil war. The Missionaries of Charity provided feeding centers for the refugees.

A BORDER SHE COULD NOT CROSS

At almost the same time as the tragedy in Calcutta and Bangladesh, Mother Teresa was living her own personal anguish, unable to change circumstances that must have tormented her. Even with world renown, Mother Teresa was unable to see her mother and sister. Her sister Aga wrote to Lazar on December 4, 1971:

> Dear ones: we are about the same; Mother is weak from her illness. I would so love to be close to you to help you and be happy together. On New Year's eve I shall be close to you in thought and heart, just as I am sure you two think of mother and Aga.
>
> I did not hear from Agnes. It seems she does not remember us any more, with all she has to do. When you write to her greet her in my name too. Mamma and Aga.[55]

With her mother asking only to see her once more, Mother Teresa again begged the Albanian embassy in Rome to grant

News from Albania

On May 4, 1973, which was during the year after the death of Aga Bojaxhiu, Mother Teresa and Eileen Egan visited Lazar in Rome. His comments on a clipping from an Italian newspaper, quoted in Such a Vision of the Street, *help to explain the separation of the family.*

"This is what is happening in Albania. A priest has been shot for baptizing a baby. His name was Father Stephan Kurti, and he was a distant relative of ours. The sister of our grandmother married a Kurti. He was imprisoned after the war as an anti-Communist and then freed for good conduct. In 1965 over two thousand mosques, churches and religious buildings, Orthodox and Catholic, were demolished or used as warehouses or museums. For protesting the demolition of Catholic churches, he was imprisoned again. A woman in the prison camp, who had given birth to a child, asked him to baptize it in secret. He agreed, even though by the law of 1967, this could be dangerous to his life. He was tried by a 'people's tribune' in a desecrated Catholic Church.

The Albanian or Italian partisans would have killed me except for my wife. When the Americans liberated Italy, I went to an American colonel and said, 'I am a colonel of a surrendered army. I can work for you. I can drive a car. He made me his jeep driver and I earned 250,000 lire (about $350) a month.'"

her entry. Leaders from around the world, including President John F. Kennedy, French president Charles de Gaulle, UN secretary general U Thant, and India's Indira Gandhi, lent their voices in petition, but all of their efforts were in vain. Mother Teresa responded stoically, saying, "Up to now I have succeeded in obtaining everything with love and prayer, but there are still barriers and obstacles that even love does not succeed in breaking down."[56]

Drana died on July 12, 1972, without seeing either her son, Lazar, or Mother Teresa. Aga's death followed shortly afterward on August 25, 1973.

Christians Serving Hindus

The personal pain of not being able to cross into Albania contrasted with the success of her efforts to cross the barriers of religion and social class. She and the Missionaries of Charity gave an impartial response to anyone in need, whatever their faith or walk of life.

For Bengali Hindus, for example, the sisters were embodiments of their most cherished values. The ideal of devout Hindus, writes biographer B. Srinivasa Murthy, is to "overcome any turmoil and challenge in life by fulfilling one's moral obligations and leaving the rest to God." For "when actions are elevated to the level of consecration to God, all actions become holy and work itself becomes a form of devotion."[57] It made no difference, especially to poor Hindus, that the sisters were Christians. The missionaries' joy and manner of work, carried on in serenity, proved them above all politics or desire for personal gain.

It was hard for some people to believe that Mother Teresa and her missionaries were acting solely for love of helping; perhaps they were trying to make converts of those they served. Mother Teresa spoke to biographer Desmond Doig about this issue of religious belief:

Oh, I hope I am converting. I don't mean what you think. I hope we are converting hearts. Not even almighty God can convert a person unless that person wants it. What we are all trying to do by our work, by serving the people, is to come closer to God. If in coming face to face with God we accept Him in our lives, then we are converting. We become a better Hindu, a better Muslim, a better Catholic, a better whatever we are, and then by being better we come closer and closer to Him. If we accept Him fully in our lives, then that is conversion. What approach would I use? For me, naturally, it would be a Catholic one, for you it may be Hindu, for someone else, Buddhist, according to one's conscience. What God is in your mind you must

Mother Teresa and her sisters succeeded in crossing the barriers of religion and social class by providing assistance to anyone in need, regardless of their race, faith, or walk of life.

accept. But I cannot prevent myself from trying to give you what I have.

I am not afraid to say I am in love with Jesus because He is everything to me. But you may have a different picture in your life. And this is the way that conversion has to be understood—people think that conversion is just changing overnight. It is not like that. Nobody, not even your father or your mother can make you do that. Not even almighty God can force a person.[58]

To those who watched and listened, Mother Teresa's self-giving was boundless. The combination of overwhelming tragedy and the example of the sisters' selfless service in the face of that tragedy multiplied Mother Teresa's many volunteers, building the missionaries' ability to address the crushing needs of Calcutta and, increasingly, of the world.

Mother Teresa kneels to kiss a statuette of Jesus after being awarded the Pope John XXIII Peace Prize in 1971.

AWARDS HELP ACHIEVE NEW LEVELS OF SERVICE

The early 1970s brought more than just humanitarian disasters. As a direct result of worldwide publicity, Mother Teresa's work was recognized in a stream of awards and honors. On January 6, 1971, she received the Pope John XXIII Peace Prize, given by Pope Paul VI, and, in September, the National Catholic Development Conference, based in Boston, Massachusetts, gave her the Good Samaritan Award. The John F. Kennedy International Award, given the next month, provided the fifteen thousand dollars needed to start the Nirmala Kennedy Centre for children with physical and mental disabilities.

Other honors followed in quick succession. On October 28, 1971, the Catholic University of America in Washington, D.C., granted her an honorary degree, doctor of humane letters.

In 1972 she received the Jawaharlal Nehru Award for International Understanding from the Indian government. This was followed in April of 1973 by the Templeton Award for Progress in Religion and the Mater et Magistra Award given by the Third Order of St. Francis in America.

SHANTINAGAR

One project that always needed funds was Shantinagar, the village for victims of leprosy. The Pope John XXIII Peace Prize of 1971 provided a boost to the entrepreneurial spirit of its director, Sister Francis Xavier. Schools were built where the lepers could learn trades such as carpentry and poultry farming to support themselves and contribute to village life. A methane gas plant engineered by the patients soon began to provide cooking fuel to the village. The village fishpond, orchard, wheat fields, and vegetable gardens, irrigated with water from the nearby Mekhand Dam, provided a constant food supply. When some used looms were given to the village, a building to house them was constructed, providing some residents with the work of weaving all the saris worn by the Missionaries of Charity.

Sister Francis Xavier's strict oversight and cheery spirit kept the village scrupulously clean so that families could live together without fear of contaminating uninfected relatives. With beautiful surroundings and meaningful work, the lepers lived with dignity.

HELP WITH HER TRAVELS TO REMOTE MISSIONS

Frequent trips to open and oversee new missions were now taking Mother Teresa in every direction, both inside and outside of the country. On August 15, 1972, a mission opened in Mauritius, an island nation located in the Indian Ocean. In 1973 she established missions in the Gaza Strip, between Egypt and Israel, in Yemen, in Australia, and in Peru.

The cost of the necessary airplane tickets seemed such a waste when the money

Indira Gandhi, prime minister of India, gave an Air India pass to Mother Teresa so that money that could be going to help the poor would not be spent on airline tickets.

could have been spent for the poor, however, so Mother Teresa decided to ask the Indian government if she could work for the airlines as a flight attendant in order to earn her tickets. Hearing of this, Indira Gandhi, the prime minister of India, presented her with a free pass on Air India so that she could supervise the worldwide activities of the missionaries.

A glimpse of the kind of travel now involved in Mother Teresa's many travels throughout India, as well as her trips abroad to open foreign missions and receive awards, comes from a letter to her spiritual sister, Jacqueline deDecker. She

wrote, "Your letter is a very great joy to me, and also strength. Because of you I am able to spend eight nights in the train and work during the day"[59]

A BRIEF MINISTRY IN NORTHERN IRELAND

Despite her rapidly spreading renown, some locations proved impossible for the Missionaries of Charity to operate in. Ironically, in the country where the Sisters of Loreto gave Mother Teresa her first lessons as a postulant, violence between Catholics and Protestants was causing much misery. As she searched for ways to reach more of the world's destitute, the plight of Northern Ireland called her back there to an area of direct combat. In *Miracle of Love*, Kathryn Spink recounts the short life of that mission, to which four sisters traveled in 1971—a place, she notes, "where hatred was preached even from the church pulpits." The situation prompted the following Co-Workers of Mother Teresa newsletter article:

> The four Sisters, equipped with two blankets each and a violin, were to take up residence in the Catholic "ghetto" of Ballymurphy—in a Council [low-income] house, which had previously been occupied by Father Hugh Mullan, a curate of the parish. The house was now empty because Father Mullan had been shot dead by "the forces of law and order" as he had just finished administering Extreme Unction to a wounded man.

This is the kind of mad situation in which the Sisters now find themselves, into which they will try to bring some spark of love, forgiveness and understanding. . . .

The house was completely empty, bereft of all furniture. It had also been ransacked by vandals while it was standing tenantless. Mother Teresa said that the two neighbouring houses had also been rented by the parish. She plans to have a small group of Anglican nuns working with her own Sisters there—a sign of unity in a strife-torn city.[60]

Within a few months, the children and elderly had begun to find the sisters' house a refuge from violence. But suddenly church officials, giving no reasons, asked them to leave; obedient to her superiors, Mother Teresa saw to it that the sisters were withdrawn.

HELPING DROUGHT VICTIMS IN ETHIOPIA

Even as one mission was closed down, however, another one opened. Hearing that drought was causing increased misery in Ethiopia, Mother Teresa went to Addis Ababa, the nation's capital, to investigate. At the time, in 1973, she knew it would be difficult to start a mission there: many other organizations had been denied similar permission. But she was encouraged when Emperor Haile Selassie's daughter arranged an audience with her father.

The audience with Emperor Selassie was very positive, brief, and to the point. The emperor told Mother Teresa, "I have heard about the good work you do. I am very happy you have come. Yes, let your Sisters come to Ethiopia."[61]

Without further ado, Sister Frederica, who had served in Belfast, was left in

British troops move in to quell the riots raging in Northern Ireland between Catholics and Protestants. Mother Teresa sent sisters to the area in 1971 to help those affected by the violence. Church officials, however, unexpectedly asked the sisters to leave after just a few months.

Addis Ababa to arrange plumbing for a house that a local business owner provided free of charge. By the time three other sisters arrived at the end of the week, the house was furnished with three tables, four beds, a gas cooker, a cupboard, and a bench.

In a note of consolation to her Co-Workers in Ireland, Mother Teresa wrote:

> Leaving Belfast was a very big sacrifice—but very fruitful—for the Sisters are now going to Ethiopia to feed the hungry Christ. The same Sisters who so lovingly served him in Belfast will now be giving his love and compassion to the suffering people of Ethiopia—pray for them and share with them the joy of loving and serving.[62]

Emperor Haile Selassie invited Mother Teresa to start a mission in Ethiopia.

NO TIME TO REST

Traveling or speaking, there were no borders too far away, no boundaries Mother Teresa was unwilling to cross in pursuit of her goals. Recognizing that such single-mindedness could well put her in physical danger, journalist Desmond Doig once asked her if she had ever had any doubts about crossing over from teaching at Loreto Entally to serving derelicts in Calcutta's slums. She answered this way:

> No, there was no doubt. . . . The moment you accept, the moment you surrender yourself, that's the conviction. But it may mean death to you, eh? The conviction comes the moment you surrender yourself. Then there is no doubt. The moment Jesus said, "Father, I am at your disposal, Thy will be done," He had accepted. That was His agony. He felt all the things you and I would feel as human beings. [And if uncertainty remains?] That is the time to go on your knees.[63]

The pace of directing the missionaries' activities was beginning to take its toll. The busy year 1973 brought the end of Mother Teresa's first term as mother general, and she wrote to the sisters that she wanted to resign from the highest position of the order, citing her many travels and her increasingly frail health. But her sisters voted to have her continue as mother general. Reluctantly, she agreed.

As her second term as the missionaries' leader opened, Mother Teresa decided it was time to address a necessity she saw among the sisters themselves—the endur-

Mother Teresa visits with children during her 1971 visit to Belfast. Unceasing travels and activities were beginning to take a toll on her health.

ing need for prayer. Toward this end, she established a number of sister relationships with contemplative communities; that is, with groups of nuns living in convents for the purpose of prayer alone. She wanted each of her congregation's houses to be "spiritually adopted" by contemplative sisters of one or another order, which would serve as powerhouses of spiritual energy.

A Silver Anniversary

In the midst of all of her other activities, Mother Teresa somehow found time to plan the celebration for the twenty-fifth anniversary of the founding of the Missionaries of Charity. In keeping with her philosophy, the poor were to be included in the celebration. A series of detailed instructions for the day, October 7, 1975, re-

quested that in each of the order's houses they were to have "a High Mass of thanksgiving and invite all our benefactors and our poor to join with us to say thank you to God for all he has done for us and for our Society these twenty-five years."[64] The celebrations were to be simple and faithful to the intent of thanksgiving. There were to be no concerts or speeches, brochures, pamphlets, or photographs. And above all, there was to be no fund-raising.

Brothers Go Overseas

Even as she oversaw all of the activities of the Missionaries of Charity, Mother Teresa continued her spiritual relationship with the Missionary Brothers of Charity. As with the sisters, her goal was to have the brothers at work among the poor throughout the world. Also like the Missionaries of Charity, the brothers shared the poverty of those they served.

One of the first overseas missions of the Missionary Brothers of Charity had been to civil-war ravaged Vietnam, where the Brothers had begun their work on February 27, 1973. Life in the underworld of Saigon, on back streets where even most Vietnamese had never ventured, was hard. One of the brothers described their house in Saigon this way:

> The first floor sleeps about thirty or so of the shelterless people. The second floor is the same but has room for classes during the day. The third floor is for the Brothers. It consists of two small rooms in which we eat, sleep, read and pray. Each Brother has a sleeping pallet like the ones the people use and this is rolled up during the day. There is no privacy and always much noise. We feed over a hundred people a day in the house. The transition has been easy for me, thank God, although the hardest thing to accept is the rats. Rain has driven them indoors and we can hear and feel them running around the floor at night.[65]

A continued presence in Vietnam was not to be, however. With the reunification of the nation under rule by the north, the brothers were ordered by the government to leave Saigon and were deported. Inspired by the example and encouragement of Mother Teresa, the brothers went on to other countries. They grew quickly

until their list of missions included Taiwan, Korea, Guatemala, Haiti, the Philippines, El Salvador, the United States, the Dominican Republic, Brazil, Madagascar, and France.

ANN BLAIKIE'S CO-WORKER ORGANIZATION

In addition to the relationship with the Missionary Brothers, Mother Teresa worked to keep other relationships maintained, always with the goal of serving the poor. The Co-Workers of Mother Teresa had continued to benefit from Ann Blaikie's organizational help for more than twenty years. After Ann's husband died in 1974, this tireless woman gave even more devotion to the network of helpers. She was now maintaining a central office from which she made certain that groups and individuals were contacted regularly with news of Mother Teresa's activities. She reproduced and distributed Mother Teresa's inspirational letters. From this office she relayed offers of help, stories of devotion, and donations.

As the years went on, Mother Teresa's relationship with the Co-Workers became more and more an attempt to bridge the gap between religious and secular life. Mother Teresa's hope was to establish for everyone a common ground of spirituality. This was not always easy for Mother Teresa personally, as each additional Co-Worker and every volunteer group, helping organization, and coalition needed to hear speeches and receive letters of inspiration from her.

SACRIFICES FROM THOSE WITH LITTLE RESOURCES

Mother Teresa was fond of stories that told of little sacrifices made by ordinary people. These anecdotes are excerpted from A Simple Path.

"The other day I received a letter from a small child in America. I knew he was little because he wrote in big handwriting, 'Mother Teresa I love you so much I'm sending you my pocket money.' And inside the letter there was a check for three dollars. Also, one of the sisters in London told me that, one day, a little girl came to the door of the home in Kilburn with a bag of pennies and she said, 'This is for the poor men.' She didn't say, 'This is for Mother Teresa': or 'for the Missionaries of Charity.' She lived down the road and had seen all the residents walking around—and so she said, 'This is for the men.' She'd just seen with her eyes and I think it's like that for so many people. They see something and they're attracted towards it because it's good.

A young couple got married here recently. They decided to keep their wedding simple—she wore a plain cotton sari and there were just his and her parents' present—and they gave us all the money they had saved from not having a big Hindu wedding ceremony. They were sharing their love with the poor. Something like this happens every day. By becoming poor ourselves, by loving until it hurts, we become capable of loving more deeply, more beautifully, more wholly.'"

Mother Teresa's message increasingly emphasized the universal nature of her mission. Poverty, she said, was experienced universally, not only by starving people in Calcutta. Poverty was loneliness, unwantedness, and unloving attitudes, and these conditions, Mother Teresa argued, were everywhere.

People around the world needed to be like her own missionaries, Mother Teresa maintained. Seeing what is directly in front of them, looking neither to the right nor to the left, taking care of the present need, they would come to know that even the smallest gift of love is priceless.

To illustrate her point, she told the following story of what might be considered reverse giving:

A beggar said, "Mother Teresa, everybody's giving to you, I also want to give to you. Today, for the whole day, I got only twenty-nine paise [100 paise = one rupee] and I want to give it to you." I thought for a moment: If I

Mother Teresa receives an honorary doctorate at Delhi University, just one of the many universities that conferred this honor upon her.

take it he will have nothing to eat tonight, and if I don't take it I will hurt him. So I put out my hands and I took the money. I have never seen such joy on anybody's face as I saw on his—that a beggar, too, could give to Mother Teresa. It was a big sacrifice for that poor man who'd been sitting in the sun all day and had only received twenty-nine paise. It was beautiful: twenty-nine paise is such a small amount and I can get nothing with it, but as he gave it up and I took it, it became like thousands because it was given with so much love.[66]

No End to the Awards

The measure of Mother Teresa's impact on the world's conscience came from still more awards she accepted in the name of the poor. She received the Albert Schweitzer International Prize from the University of North Carolina. The FAO Ceres Medal from the United Nations Food and Agriculture Organization was given to her in Rome in 1975.

Other recognition came in the form of honorary degrees. When, in 1976, the University of Santiniketan-Visva-Bharati conferred on her an honorary degree,

SIDELIGHTS ON KALIGHAT'S NIRMAL HRIDAY

Sister Dolores, working at Nirmal Hriday, observed that the missionaries try to address the immediate needs of those who come to them. She describes some aspects of their work in A Simple Path, *compiled by Lucinda Vardey.*

"We never ask people why they are on the street: we don't need to know their history. We don't judge them for whatever situation they are in, because all they want is some love and care and they are satisfied. We just look after the person who is brought to us and God does the rest through us.

What usually happens when a person arrives is that she or he is given a bath. But sometimes a person is so ill that we just give her a bed, wash her face, and put her on an IV drip. Sometimes we need to care for those with gangrene or bad wounds with maggots or chronic diarrhea. Many arrive with TB and some are bleeding—the bleeding must be stopped first of all.

Sometimes, as soon as a patient lies on the bed she dies. At other times, patients get a little better, can sit up in bed or stand or walk about, and some of them go back home, although home for many is just the street. So some leave us and then return if they get sick again. We say we will keep a bed for them."

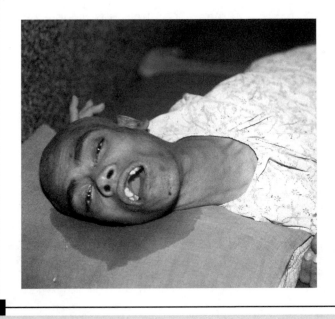

The patients at Nirmal Hriday receive loving care and compassion from the sisters, who do not judge them or ask them about their past history.

Prime Minister Indira Gandhi presided over the ceremony. In 1977 an honorary degree from Cambridge University in England was conferred on her by Britain's Prince Philip. Characteristically wishing to remind the world of the poor, Mother Teresa went to receive her honors wearing her sari and with only rough sandals on her feet.

MISSIONS CONTINUE TO OPEN

There seemed no end to Mother Teresa's energy in starting new ministries. But each new mission awoke in her a greater sense of her own poverty and helplessness. As ever, she turned to prayer to supply what she needed. She followed up her earlier idea of pairing her missions with contemplative communities. She opened the first foundation of the Missionaries of Charity, Contemplative, where the sisters would "live the word of God in Eucharistic adoration and contemplation."[67] This meant that through prayer and participation in communion, these sisters would provide spiritual support to those who worked directly with the poor.

The chapel in which her first contemplatives would spend their days and nights of constant prayer was part of a rededicated convent in the parish of St. Anthony of Padua in the Bronx in New York. The contemplatives were governed by rules that emphasized austerity and prayer. But, in contrast to the traditional contemplative communities, they set aside two hours a day for visiting the sick and dying. Also, they could invite women from the area to join them in the convent for days of shared prayer.

Energized by this new source of spiritual support, the Missionaries of Charity opened seven new international missions in 1978—Syhlet, Bangladesh; Metro Manila, Philippines; Caracas, Venezuela; Zárate, Argentina; Liverpool, England;

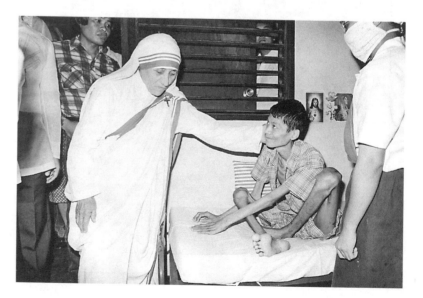

Mother Teresa comforts a polio victim at her mission in Manila, one of seven new missions opened by the Missionaries of Charity in 1978 alone.

A Volunteer Tells How He Benefited

Mother Teresa could be subtle in the way she taught volunteers to deal with those in need. In A Simple Path, *compiled by Lucinda Vardey, one of the volunteers tells how he learned the way of the poor.*

"A little bug used to be in my ear saying, 'You've got to do something for God.' I had no idea what to do. Then I saw an item in our parish bulletin that said: 'Wanted, young man to help nuns in South Bronx in young men's shelter.' So I gave them a ring and went down there. I said, 'Sister, I'm looking for the shelter,' and she said, 'Go round the corner.' She obviously assumed I needed help. The sisters have a rule that we take in the people from last night first and all new people wait until the very end. So here I am, I'm looking at all these helpless, homeless drug addicts, alcoholics, and I go walking right up front when they open the door and they say, 'Please wait.' So I think, All right, I'll wait—and I get back in my car, because it's a little chilly. People are standing out there and after about three times and them telling me to still wait, I'm getting irked—maybe I'll pack it in. It's cold, getting dark, and I'm thinking, What am I standing here for? I'm the last one.

Finally I ring the bell. They open the door and I say, 'My name is Gerry, I've come to volunteer.' They say, 'Oh, we've been waiting for you!' and that's when I knew they had me, because the sister said, 'You've been in the cold with the poor.' And I've been at that door twice a week now for thirteen years. Every time I have to tell a guy to wait, 'Just be patient,' I'm always very conscious of how that feels."

Tabora, Tanzania; and El Dorado, Panama. The following year, after eight years of effort, missions were opened in Zagreb and in Mother Teresa's hometown of Skopje, along with another fifteen overseas missions—from Beirut, Lebanon, to Detroit, Michigan. Now the missionaries' houses totaled two hundred worldwide and sixty in Calcutta. A short time later a second and a third contemplative house were opened in Brooklyn, New York, and in Anacostia, Maryland, located near Washington, D.C.

The pace of Mother Teresa's life was beginning to wear on her as she approached her seventieth year. She wanted to step down from her position as mother general and have more time for prayer and for simply visiting her people around the world. When the required general chapter of her order met in 1979, she wrote another letter of resignation and left the election open to nominations. The representatives to the general chapter again responded by reelecting her.

A NEW INSIGHT TO POVERTY

As Mother Teresa's contacts increasingly brought her to developed nations, she became motivated by a new insight—that the unwanted and unloved in places like London and New York were no better off than India's poorest of the poor. One observer writes,

> Visiting London the winter of 1979, Mother Teresa found old men sleeping in Trafalgar Square. In Covent Garden a heroin addict fell at her feet,

dying of an overdose of barbituates. "Look in your own homes, down your own streets," she told her Co-Workers, "and bring the love of God to people as the brothers and sisters would do if they were here."[68]

With this expansion of her vision, Mother Teresa began encouraging people of the developed nations to find the poverty at their own front door.

THE NOBEL PEACE PRIZE: THE CLIMAX OF A DECADE

As her vision of the needs of the poor widened, so too did Mother Teresa's renown. During the 1970s Mother Teresa received fifteen major international awards for humanitarian service. Then, late in 1979 came announcement that she had been awarded the greatest honor of all, the Nobel Peace Prize.

Chapter

6 A Peacemaker Above Politics (1979–1991)

Mother Teresa, accompanied by her two most senior Missionaries of Charity, Sister Agnes and Sister Gertrude, along with Eileen Egan, spent four historic days, December 8–12, 1979, in Oslo, Norway. They joined in processions to the Catholic and Lutheran churches, walked in a candlelight parade, had their pictures taken, and answered interviewers' questions in local events preceding the Nobel ceremonies. They visited with Mother Teresa's brother, Lazar Bojaxhiu, and with Jacqueline deDecker, who came for the presentation ceremony. But the sisters never deviated from their devotion to the poor.

Having already, in her mind, spent the $190,000 prize money on the poor, Mother Teresa and her companions held to their policy of never eating out. Indeed, Mother Teresa even convinced the Nobel committee to cancel the awards banquet, another $6,300, so that she could give that money as well to the poor. In response to this gesture, young people in Norway and other places in the world spontaneously gave another $75,600.

At the presentation ceremony, the chairman of the Norwegian Nobel Committee, Professor John Sannes, introduced Mother Teresa and spoke of her philosophy:

> In her eyes the person who, in the accepted sense, is the recipient, is also the giver and the one who gives the most. Giving—giving something of oneself—is what confers real joy, and the person who is allowed to give is the one who receives the most precious gift. Where others see clients or customers, she sees fellow-workers, a relationship based not on the expectation of gratitude on the one part, but on mutual understanding and respect, and a warm human and enriching contact.[69]

An hour-long acceptance speech on peace in the world was next on the agenda. Not wasting time with formal preparation and focused on making the most of the opportunity to draw attention to the needy, Mother Teresa spoke without notes. Undaunted by the glittering audience in black tie and formal dress, she began by asking everyone to join her in praying, "Lord, make me an instrument of your peace."

In her address, she touched on various concerns: women and the family in society, poverty and injustice as the worst enemies

Mother Teresa is presented with the 1979 Nobel Peace Prize. At her request, money designated for the awards banquet was given to the poor.

of peace, and of her hope for love among all peoples. She gave examples of sacrificial giving. "A little four-year-old," she told the audience, "went home and said to his parents: 'I don't want to eat any sugar for three days; I want to give it to Mother Teresa.'"[70]

AN UNWANTED SUBJECT

After her usual anecdotes about giving to and receiving from the poor, the sick, and the dying, Mother Teresa addressed a topic that many found controversial. She launched into her chief message, con-

demning the use of abortion as a means of birth control.

Every child, she contended, was sacred. The worst threat to world peace was to destroy children's safety in the family by abortion. She went on to give her idea of alternatives to abortion:

> We are fighting abortion by adoption, we have saved thousands of lives, we have sent words to all the clinics, to the hospitals, police stations—please don't destroy the child, we will take the child. So every hour of the day and night it is always somebody, we have quite a number of unwedded

mothers—tell them come, we will take care of you, we will take the child from you, and we will get a home for the child. And we have a tremendous demand [from] families who have no children, that is the blessing of God for us. And also, we are doing another thing which is very beautiful—we are teaching our beggars, our leprosy patients, our slum dwellers, our people of the street, natural family planning. And in Calcutta alone in six years—it is all in Calcutta—we have had 61,273 babies less from the families who would have had, but because they practise this natural way of abstaining, of self-control, out of love for each other. . . . And you know what they have told me? Our family is healthy, our family is united, and we can have a baby whenever we want.[71]

The audience listened quietly, and although Mother Teresa's decision to speak out on abortion may have caused discomfort for some, there was wide agreement that the 1979 Nobel Peace Prize was an appropriate recognition of her work.

As for herself, all she wanted was quiet and time for prayer. Hoping simply to resume her routine, Mother Teresa returned home, where bands greeted her and receptions awaited. Only the second Nobel laureate in India's history, she was the darling of the Calcutta media. But letters, telegrams, telephone calls, and photographers did not keep her from her month-long retreat at the motherhouse.

Mother Teresa, who believed that abortion is a serious threat to world peace, speaks to a right-to-life group in California.

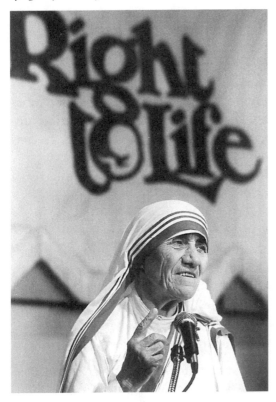

HEADS OF GOVERNMENT JOIN THE PEACE EFFORT

The pride that her adopted country took in Mother Teresa was reflected in the awarding of the Bharat Ratna (Jewel of India). In presenting the award, Indian president N. Sanjiva Reddy characterized Mother Teresa as a reflection of the nation's values, established at the time of independence.

Outside of India, Mother Teresa took her role as peacemaker seriously, carrying the Indian way abroad, a way foreign to most

Mother Teresa meets with Queen Elizabeth of England, one of the many world leaders whose support and cooperation she earned.

By her insistence that international expansion of the Missionaries of Charity, and the recognition of its founder, must transcend government authority, Mother Teresa was able to go where political, even humanitarian, services could not. Being the head of a papal congregation meant that she had the pope's blessing to go anywhere that there were poor and needy people; that is, into every country. She considered the world her backyard. As she told a journalist at the Nobel Peace Prize ceremony, "By blood and origin, I am an Albanian. My citizenship is Indian. I am a Catholic nun. As to my calling, I belong to the whole world. As to my heart, I belong entirely to the heart of Jesus."[73]

FROM LEPROSY TO AIDS

Mother Teresa's thoughts were seldom far from her ministry to lepers, especially in Calcutta, where social barriers against lepers continued strong. Soon, her defense for lepers extended to other diseases that caused their victims to be outcasts.

Calling AIDS the leprosy of the West, Mother Teresa saw AIDS ministry as work ideally suited for the missionaries. With the help of Cardinal John O'Connor, she transcended the politics of New York City and founded a hospice for victims of AIDS in Greenwich Village. She named her new ministry Gift of Love.

Mother Teresa characterized those who came to Gift of Love as being

usually the ones who were rejected or who had nobody and carried a lot of

peacemakers. To characterize "the Indian way," biographer Navin Chawla compares Mother Teresa's approach to Gandhi's: "While the Mahatma [Gandhi] was a man spurred by impulses that went beyond politics, Mother Teresa eschews politics completely."[72] This neutrality and tolerance enabled her to ask for and get cooperation from persons with drastically differing political views, from U.S. presidents Ronald Reagan and George Bush to the royalty of England and even to dictators of both Communist and Fascist countries.

GOVERNOR JERRY BROWN VOLUNTEERS AT KALIGHAT

In the early 1980s Jerry Brown, the then-governor of California, studied Buddhism in Japan and then began to think of Mother Teresa as "the perfect embodiment of enlightenment: love of God expressed directly by serving the poorest of the poor." To make this insight real to himself, he volunteered to spend three weeks at Kalighat. Here is an excerpt of what he told his father afterward, published in Life *magazine.*

"One young boy was brought in off the streets with the skin of his right hand completely burned away. The yellow tendons were exposed. Each time the nurse tried to clean the wound, he screamed. A week later an Australian nurse and I took him to a hospital where a doctor volunteered to perform a skin graft. I asked the nurse what would have happened if the sisters hadn't taken him in. 'He would have died of infection,' she replied. 'It is as simple as that. . . .'

To work with the dying and destitute—getting a person a glass of water, helping with a bedpan—is to encounter life at a very basic level: People can be surprisingly happy and grateful when you help them with even the smallest things. In Calcutta I experienced a directness and immediacy that I have rarely encountered elsewhere. You see the gratitude or the pain on faces. Nothing is filtered by a need to impress anyone. . . .

The Sunday before I left, Mother Teresa visited Kalighat. She leaned down next to a man whose hand I was holding and put her face close to his. She paused and tried to comfort him. She told me he was saying, 'God, God, take me! take me!' His lungs were full of fluid. The pain seemed excruciating. Two hours later he died. . . .

I could not imagine that a president would be treated better than these forgotten people. This is what got to me: the dignity given people who had absolutely nothing. What a world it would be if somehow this became the predominant spirit."

California governor Jerry Brown talks with Mother Teresa, whose works inspired him to spend three weeks volunteering amongst the poor in Calcutta.

bitterness in their hearts. Coping with the last stages of life is hard, so we'd take time to create a family spirit among them—we'd eat together, talk, play, and pray together. Many were not close to their families, but after being with us for a while, and through the gift of God, they'd be brought together with their parents. Some would write letters and others would telephone. And, as we grew, one sick man would take care of another—which was always wonderful to witness.[74]

Mother Teresa meets with Mayor Ed Koch to ask him for assistance with her New York AIDS ministry. The Missionaries of Charity opened a number of AIDS hospices.

Soon the Missionaries of Charity had opened five more homes dedicated to the care of people suffering from AIDS.

But the opening of the AIDS hospice, along with Mother Teresa's acceptance of the Medal of Freedom from President Ronald Reagan, became the focus of increasingly frequent comments about the contradictions she presented in the West.

THE MEDAL OF FREEDOM

After the presentation of the Medal of Freedom in June 1988, these contradictions were expressed publicly. Two freelance writers, Peggy Noonan in *Time* and Stephanie Harrington in *Ms.*, presented opposing opinions regarding Mother Teresa's message. Noonan wrote of her encounter with Mother Teresa at the White House:

> What a sight: a saint in a sari coming down the White House hall. As she came nearer, I could not help it: I bowed. "Mother," I said, "I just want to touch your hand." She looked up at me—it may have been one of God's subtle jokes that his exalted child spent her life looking up to everyone else—and said only two words. Later I would realize that they were the message of her mission. *"Luff Gott,"* she said. Love God. She pressed into my hand a poem she had written as she glided away in a swoosh of habit.[75]

Stephanie Harrington, on the other hand, pointed to the contradiction that Mother Teresa presented:

Mother Teresa speaks at the White House in 1985, pictured here with President Ronald Reagan and the First Lady. In 1988, President Reagan presented Mother Teresa with the Medal of Freedom.

[The] same religious conviction that inspires them [the Missionaries of Charity] to give succor to victims of the disease [AIDS] demands that they oppose the primary means . . . to prevent its spread from one person to another or from pregnant woman to fetus: contraception and abortion.[76]

For Harrington, Mother Teresa's unquestioning obedience to such directives of her Catholic religion (no artificial birth control, no abortion) conflicted with the values of others who were trying to relieve the suffering of the world.

THE SOUTH AFRICAN MISSION

All contradictions aside, every door closed by politics or diplomacy or social barrier beckoned Mother Teresa to find a way to open it. Thus, she eventually tackled another country that denied entrance to outside missionaries. The challenge was to bring a message of reconciliation to the Republic of South Africa, a country deeply divided over the racist policy of apartheid. Mother Teresa said that she did not understand apartheid. In her words, "White, black, green, yellow, whatever, you are all children of God, created for greater things, to love and to be loved."[77]

In November 1988 Mother Teresa managed to gain entrance to South Africa and set to work. She chose for the site of her mission the township Khayelitsha, located among the sand dunes near Cape Town and populated by mixed-race people designated by their government as "colored." Mother Teresa insisted that she chose that location only because its people were poor, not because they were nonwhite. She followed her usual practice in searching for a new home for a mission: She prayed. Biographer Kathryn Spink recounts,

While in Cape Town, South Africa, Mother Teresa is greeted warmly by Archbishop Desmond Tutu. The Sisters of Charity were the first missionaries allowed access to South Africa, where the racist policy of apartheid had polarized the nation.

On Wednesday, 9 November Mother Teresa prayed to St. Joseph that she would find a convent for her nuns in Khayelitsha, and by lunchtime her prayer had been answered. . . . The Sisters would be moving into what had been a home for the elderly owned by the Catholic Welfare Bureau. They would move in that very evening and spend the night there. Eventually she would like a little more land to build a place for the sick and the dying, but for the moment the Sisters' needs had been met.[78]

HEALTH SETBACKS TO THE WORK OF MOTHER TERESA

Political boundaries proved surmountable for Mother Teresa, but by the mid-1980s she was facing a far more tenacious opponent, age. Beginning in 1983 Mother Teresa increasingly had been plagued by injuries and other health problems. During a physical examination occasioned by a fall from bed, doctors discovered heart disease. To forestall a severe heart attack, doctors inserted a pacemaker to encourage a regular heartbeat.

The fact that she had received the pacemaker presented a contradiction to some people. Critics noted that she was benefiting from treatment not ordinarily available to the poor. Mother Teresa, however, took her recovery as a sign of God's will that she should continue her work.

As a concession to her failing health, however, Mother Teresa petitioned the pope to allow the election for mother general to be held a year early. She wrote to the sisters requesting retirement. At the general chapter, however, the sisters

Two European Missionaries Meet

In City of Joy, Dominique Lapierre tells of how his friend the Polish priest Stephan Kovalski met Mother Teresa at Nirmal Hriday in Kalighat when he came to ask for a mobile unit to serve the lepers in Anand Nagar, the slum where he lived.

"[Kovalski] made his way between the rows of bodies and approached a kneeling figure. The nun was bathing the wounds of a man who was still young but who was so thin that he looked like one of the living dead discovered by the Allies in the Nazi concentration camps. All his flesh had melted away. Only his skin remained, stretched taut over his bones. The woman was speaking softly to him in Bengali.

'I shall never forget that man's expression,' Kovalski was to say. 'His suffering was transformed into surprise, then peace, the peace that comes from being loved.' Sensing a presence behind her, Mother Teresa stood up. She did not fail to notice the metal cross the visitor was wearing on his chest.

'Oh Father,' she excused herself humbly, 'what can I do for you?'

Stephan Kovalski felt awkward. He had just interrupted a conversation in which he identified something unique. The eyes of the dying man seemed to be imploring Mother Teresa to bend over him once more. It was deeply touching. The priest introduced himself.

'I think I've heard people talk about you!' she said warmly.

'Mother, I've come to ask for your help.'

'My help?' She pointed a large hand toward the ceiling. 'It's God's help you want to ask for, Father. I am nothing at all.'

At that point a young American in jeans came along carrying a bowl. Mother Teresa called him over and drew his attention to the dying man.

'Love him,' she ordered. 'Love him with all your might.' She handed the young man her tweezers and cloth and left him, steering Stephan Kovalski toward an empty area with a table and bench between the room for men and the one for women. . . . The Pole outlined his plan for a leper clinic in the City of Joy. 'Very good, Father, very good,' commented Mother Teresa in her picturesque accent, a mixture of Slavonic and Bengali. 'You are doing God's work. All right, Father, I'll send you three Sisters who are used to caring for lepers.'"

Mother Teresa and Pope John Paul II greet the thousands of followers who have gathered in Calcutta. She adhered strictly to the teachings of the pope.

once more unanimously reelected Mother Teresa.

SUPPORT FROM THE POPE

Unmoved by criticism of her stance on abortion and birth control, Mother Teresa took seriously her promise of obedience to the pope. Working with bishop after bishop in homes to care for the poor around the world, she accepted as her own the pope's positions, most publicly on teaching about abortion.

Inevitably, Mother Teresa came to the attention of the pope himself, and in 1978 she had a private audience with Pope Paul VI. And in 1986, Pope John Paul II visited India, and she herself led him around the hospice in Kalighat. Biographer Kathryn Spink narrates the event:

When the Pope arrived straight from Dum Dum airport in his Rover Popemobile, Mother Teresa stepped into the vehicle to touch his feet but he blessed her with a kiss on the forehead and a hug. Mother Teresa introduced him to the head *sevayat* [priest] of the adjacent Kali temple, and then took him to a dais erected in his honour where she garlanded him. The Pope took off the garland and placed it round her neck, and the large crowd which had gathered to greet him cheered. John Paul II spent almost three-quarters of an hour in Nirmal Hriday, feeding some of the occupants, pausing beside the low cots to hold the face of a suffering person in his hands, blessing them.[79]

A Hospice in Vatican City

Regardless of her growing influence in Rome, Mother Teresa was forced to accept delay of one project: a mission in Vatican City itself. As she and others had observed, Rome's thousands of poor citizens were spilling over into the pope's own territory, sleeping in the doorways of shops in Vatican City and under the very arches of the churches. She had asked the pope many times for permission to open a house within the walls of the Holy City, but that permission was slow in coming.

The Vatican announcement finally came in May 1987 that a home, to be called Gift of Mary, was being designed by a leading Italian architect, Angelo Malfatto. The plans located the building in a courtyard near the Vatican offices. It would have large kitchens and dining space; in addition, it would accommodate seventy-four sick and homeless people and have doors open to "all tramps and vagabonds . . . regardless of their religion, . . . to people of all faiths—and those of none."[80]

The contrast between this well-designed home and Mother Teresa's poor mission in

Lazar Bojaxhiu Renews Contact with His Sister

In Robert Serrou's biography Teresa of Calcutta, *Lazar Bojaxhiu tells how his intrepid sister could be more than a match for government officials who tried to enforce rules that impeded her mission.*

"When we were saying good-bye in Rome, I witnessed a typical incident. We were at the airport, she was leaving for Delhi. She and the other nuns with her had just been told that they couldn't carry their rough bundles with them—bundles of food, clothing, and God-knows-what that they had collected to take back to India, all wrapped up in newspapers, ragged cardboard, and strings. Piles and piles of the stuff. As I went to say good-bye to her, she and the other sisters were kneeling down in the middle of the airport—causing quite a scene, as you can imagine, with Italian customs officers everywhere waving their arms and arguing frantically with her. I asked her what was wrong. 'Oh, we're just kneeling down,' she said, 'to ask God to change the officials' mind so that we can carry these gifts to their destination.' I could hardly keep from laughing. And within three minutes two or three more uniformed officials appeared to say it would be all right after all, and to try to hurry the sisters along and get the scene over with. *That's* how she works."

Rome did not keep her from being pleased that the pope had given the poor a place in the Catholic Church's administrative heart.

BEHIND THE IRON CURTAIN AND OTHER CURTAINS

Mother Teresa's vision of peace went beyond the vision of the Nobel committee. Wherever war or oppression kept people from practicing their religion, she believed, there was a lack of peace. She had no qualms about visiting dictators in order to bring care to those they ruled. And she received awards and favors from those very rulers. The military ruler of Haiti, "Baby Doc" Duvalier and his wife, Michéle, entertained her and gave her a large sum of money, along with permission to open a mission.

Two and a half years later, Sister Carmeline wrote about their work in this poor country at the mission in Port-au-Prince:

> The first thing we did was to learn the language. One priest kindly helped us for two weeks to learn Creole and then we started to visit the poor people around us. And then we found out so many poor areas and also a place in the general hospital known as the "depot"—where we found so many sick and abandoned people waiting to get a bed, but many died before entering inside. . . . Now we have a big home for the sick and dying. About sixty patients can be taken inside, and always it is full. Besides this we have a school for the slum children. . . . About two hundred slum children receive the education in our school. Then we have four dispensaries. . . . Then we have a nutrition center attended by four hundred children daily.[81]

Other previously closed doors opened. In cooperation with the Philippine strongman, Ferdinand Marcos, the Missionaries of Charity opened missions in that country. And finally, Mother Teresa made her way into Albania, still ruled by a communist dictator.

For some years she had expressed her desire to establish a mission in the Soviet

Mother Teresa walks with a young child at the mission in Port-au-Prince, Haiti.

Brother Geoff Speaks About
Work in the East and the West

Comparisons between Western and Eastern views of how time should be used provide a sense of Mother Teresa's definition of love. Brother Geoff, the second director of the Missionary Brothers of Charity, had this comment in A Simple Path, *compiled by Lucinda Vardey.*

"In the West we have a tendency to be profit-oriented, where everything is measured according to the results and we get caught up in being more and more active to generate results. In the East—especially in India—I find that people are most content to just *be*, to just sit around under a banyan tree for half a day chatting to each other. We Westerners would probably call that wasting time. But there is value to it. Being with someone, listening without a clock and without anticipation of results, teaches us about love. The success of love is in the loving—it is not in the result of loving. Of course it is natural in love to want the best for the other person, but whether it turns out that way or not does not determine the value of what we have done. The more we can remove this priority for results the more we can learn about the contemplative element of love. There is the love expressed in the service and the love in the contemplation. It is the balance of both which we should be striving for. Love is the key to finding this balance."

Union. But it was not until December 8, 1988, that the Soviet Peace Committee, an official arm of the Soviet government, actually invited Mother Teresa to bring sisters to Moscow.

The Soviet invitation came the day after fifty-five thousand people died in a severe earthquake in Armenia, then a province of the Soviet Union. When she arrived in Moscow the next week, she was determined to send four sisters to Armenia as well.

Her stay in Moscow soon included a side trip to Armenia. By the end of her two-week stay, she not only had received the additional four sisters into their home in Spitak, Armenia, but she had also won permission for an Australian priest to enter the country and had celebrated Christmas mass with them.

As the 1990s opened, the growth of the Missionaries of Charity continued unabated. Volunteers and novices from many countries were flocking to help, making it possible to send more and more sisters to Africa, South and Central America, the United States, Scotland, and Canada.

Chapter

7 "She Was Tough" (1991–1997)

Throughout her ministry, Mother Teresa had tolerated fame and awards only for the sake of the poor. Yet, as early as the 1960s, she was recognized by filmmaker Malcolm Muggeridge as a media star. Her smile and directness, simplicity and otherworldiness appealed to the public. Her untiring desire to serve the poor was newsworthy to the end. Even her humble awareness of the countless others whose stories of selfless giving did not reach the television screens and news magazines merited quotations. For example, she once protested, "Why all this fuss about us? . . . Others do the same work as we do. Do it perhaps better. Why single us out?"[82] Her sturdy persistence brought a message of hope to the world. From *Good Housekeeping* and *Ms.* to *Newsweek* and *Time*, no periodical could afford to ignore the possibilities for audience appeal in a story about Mother Teresa.

The relationship worked both ways. Mother Teresa understood the value of publicity for her work. For example, when some people in Calcutta protested that her publicizing of the city's poverty was detrimental to the city's image, she

pointed out the response that publicity had generated:

> a hundred thousand schoolchildren in Denmark going without a glass of milk every day in order that others might eat; eight hundred thousand capsules of [the leprosy antidote] Lampren sent annually from Switzerland to the lepers in West Bengal; five thousand tons of high-quality processed food dispatched at a week's notice for the famine-stricken people of Ethiopia and Tanzania.[83]

In her view, the good results of the publicity far outweighed the bad. Publicity about Mother Teresa and her fifty-year-old order continued, even as her health failed. Sick and suffering people around the world watched the news reports on Mother Teresa, wondering if she would live through the night and praying that she would survive the latest fall or heart attack. Her tenacity cheered many. As writer Peggy Noonan later put it, "She was tough. There was the worn and weathered face, the abrupt and definite speech. We think saints are soft, ethereal, pious and meek. But some saints are steamrollers."[84]

A Remembered Blessing

Mother Teresa usually insisted that journalists spend some time volunteering among the people they wished to photograph and interview. When photojournalist Linda Schaefer was leaving Calcutta with her photographs and her memories, she received what she considered a special blessing.

"[Mother Teresa] held her hand over my head, and I felt her nurturing radiance pass through me. It was a very special moment, for I knew at that time that I was pregnant, carrying my son Paul.

I cherish the time I spent with Mother Teresa and what I learned about service to others. I'm still in contact with some of the volunteers I worked with in Calcutta, and we all feel so blessed by the weeks or months we spent near Mother Teresa. . . .

Yet, Mother Teresa herself would not have wanted to take any credit. Time after time, she insisted that she was only God's instrument. She never took credit for her works in India or saw herself as larger than life. 'It's not me,' she always insisted. Always, she insisted that the spotlight be turned toward God, rather than herself."

A photojournalist, Linda Schaefer, who traveled to Calcutta in October 1995, was granted a brief interview with the busy mother general of the Missionaries of Charity. Schaefer told Mother Teresa she wanted to document her work in Calcutta.

"I don't need photographs," Mother Teresa responded, "I need volunteers."[85] Schaefer, who was directed to Shishu Bhavan, the orphanage a few blocks from the motherhouse, took care of some of the babies and spent volunteer time at the hospice in Kalighat. Only then did Mother Teresa grant permission for her to take the pictures she sought.

Failing Health but No Compromise

As she entered her ninth decade, it was her love of life and her mission that kept Mother Teresa going, in spite of failing health. The source of her strength of will, it seemed, was the room reserved for prayer at the motherhouse. In order to sit in this room, a rosary in her hand, she defied doctors' orders to stay in the hospital or go to a nursing home. Fortified by her time there, she continued to travel far and wide, ignoring her own pain and faltering heart in order to visit missions and give talks.

Reading greeting cards from well-wishers, Mother Teresa is wheeled out of the hospital after being treated for multiple health problems. Despite her deteriorating health, she continued to visit missions and speak to audiences all over the world.

Despite failing health, she was constantly in motion. In May 1991 she left the hospital and her heart treatment to go to Bangladesh, where a hurricane had left thirty thousand dead. Then it was on to Baghdad, Iraq, in June 1991 to open a house and feeding center for disabled children. By July 1992 she had opened six houses in Albania. In Cuba she opened two houses in August 1991, another a year later in Haiti, and another that same month in the former Soviet republic of Estonia.

PRINCESS DIANA

Through her unceasing activities she attracted the attention and admiration of many famous and powerful people. Never intimidated by royalty, she accepted a request from Britain's Princess Diana to meet with her and planned Diana's visit for February 1992. When this meeting had to be called off because she suffered a heart attack just before Princess Diana was to arrive, Mother Teresa willingly rescheduled. On September 9, 1992, Princess Diana came to see her in the hospital. This was the beginning of a genuine friendship between two people who at first appeared to have little in common.

It seemed obvious to many who witnessed the meeting that Princess Diana truly admired Mother Teresa. Among journalists who commented was Michael Satchell of *U.S. News & World Report:*

There were common points in the lives of the tiny, wizened nun and the willowy, beautiful princess. . . . Adored by millions, the tragic, privileged Diana was sanctified as much for her beauty and fame as for her willingness to reject the stiff traditions of British royalty and openly embrace the sick and handicapped. Mother Teresa, whose Missionaries of Charity minister to

Sharing a common love and compassion for children and the needy, Princess Diana and Mother Teresa formed a genuine friendship after their initial meeting in 1992. Here, the two meet for what would be the last time at the Missionaries of Charity convent in the Bronx.

millions of people worldwide, was revered as a "living saint" whose lifetime of caring for the destitute and the dying earned her the Nobel Peace Prize in 1979.

The two women shared a compassion for the less fortunate and a deep love of children. Their final meeting took place last June [1996] at the Missionaries of Charity convent in the Bronx. The ailing missionary stepped out of her wheelchair to stroll with Diana. Arm in arm the pair kissed, hugged, and prayed in a scene that the British press dubbed the most remarkable royal walkabout ever.[86]

FACE-OFF ON
SOURCES OF FUNDING

Given Mother Teresa's visibility, perhaps it was inevitable that criticism of her

should surface. The public attack came in 1994 when Christopher Hitchens, a columnist with *Nation* and *Vanity Fair*, wrote a documentary titled *Hell's Angel* for Channel 4 in Great Britain. Targeting Mother Teresa's acceptance of donations from oppressive rulers and other benefactors, Hitchens questioned Mother Teresa's insistence that she was commissioned to do God's work.

In his television documentary, Hitchens criticized Mother Teresa's visits to the Soviet Union and Albania, saying that she compromised her Christian principles by consorting with dictators. Hitchens quoted Mother Teresa's favorable comments about Michéle Duvalier, wife of Haiti's dictator:

> [Mother Teresa] confirmed my suspicions by voyaging to Haiti, where the wretched of the earth are even more comprehensively ground down than they are in Calcutta, and by accepting an award from the Duvalier despotism. Of Michele Duvalier, . . . she

Mother Teresa departs with a prayerful gesture after meeting in Beijing with Deng Pufang, the son of China's top leader. She has been criticized for consorting with and accepting donations from dictators of countries such as China and the Soviet Union.

HUMANITARIANISM VS. FREE AND LOVING SERVICE

Mary Poplin, a professor of education at the Claremont Graduate School, volunteered at the children's home in Calcutta in 1996. There, she discovered how wide a range of people were served. She gives her impressions in her article "No Humanitarian," which appeared in the periodical Commonweal.

"The destitute families know the sisters understand their plight. Most of the sick infants with whom I worked had to be left with us for an extended period to get well. The parents were not afraid to admit to the sisters that they couldn't care for their children during such illnesses. Sometimes we even had healthy babies whose parents were ill or in crisis. The Missionaries do not judge these parents for their inability to take care of the infants. They do not think of poor parents as the enemies of poor children, as is too often done in this country.

To really comprehend what the sisters are about, however, it is important to understand that they do not embrace this hard life simply to better understand and serve the poor. Rather, they are poor in order to follow Christ, who chose to be poor, to be born in a stable, to live and die with no possessions. Elected poverty is a reparation, in part, for the materialistic sins of the world. Mother Teresa was firm about the source of poverty; she said, 'God does not create poverty, we do, because we do not share.' But when asked why she didn't become more involved in the politics of poverty and world hunger, she replied, 'that was not my calling. God calls others to this task. Me he just called to tend the poorest of the poor. We must each stay faithful to our own call, be faithful to the things God calls each of us to do and do them with holiness.'"

said, "I have seen many people coming, kings and people, presidents and prime ministers, but I have never seen the poor people being so familiar with their heads of state as they were with her. It was a beautiful lesson for me."[87]

Hitchens further criticized Mother Teresa for accepting $1.4 million and the use of a private jet from Charles Keating, head of the failed Lincoln Savings and Loan. In Hitchens' view, because the U.S. government had to provide money to repay customers who had lost their savings, "the money wasn't Keating's to give away."[88] The criticism grieved Mother Teresa, but she did not apologize. In her view, the donations were made in good faith and, as such, were an expression of God's care for the poor.

A CANADIAN JOURNALIST'S VIEW

At about the same time as the airing of *Hell's Angel* came the publication of Lucinda Vardey's *A Simple Path,* a collection of pithy quotations by Mother Teresa and other missionaries and volunteers. Vardey emphasized Mother Teresa's one-on-one appeal to the heart and the faith of Missionaries of Charity, Co-Workers, and volunteers. The Canadian journalist and Buddhist told interviewer Marci McDonald how she had been charmed by Mother Teresa's humanity:

> On her first day in Calcutta, [Vardey] was tickled by her subject's mix of piety and pragmatism. In the midst of predawn prayers, Mother Teresa noticed someone had left on a light. "She gathered herself up off the floor to turn it off," Vardey recounts. "I loved her right there." Her experience at the mission also had a profound personal effect: "I knew there would be a big lesson in this for me—how I put my faith into action."[89]

THE CO-WORKERS ORGANIZATION IS DISSOLVED

Ever practical, Mother Teresa was capable of making difficult choices when she felt

the interests of the poor were at stake. She had, for example, over the years, altered her outlook on collecting money. At an international meeting of the Co-Workers on May 3–7, 1993, she came to the conclusion that Co-Worker fund-raising was a spiritual danger. She worried that donations that could go to the poor might be financing Co-Workers' travels or publication of their newsletter. Consequently, she announced that the Co-Workers would no longer be an official organization: "I do not want the Co-Workers as an 'organization' to continue," she said. "I have written to all the Bishops around the world that I have made this decision."[90]

THE FINAL "UNWANTED"

Mother Teresa's term as mother general was drawing to a close. The archbishop of Calcutta announced in January 1997 that Mother Teresa wished to resign and made it plain that her wishes this time were to be honored at the general chapter.

U.S. News & World Report carried the news around the world. "Taking a Much Deserved Rest," read the headline. "Having pulled through a recent episode of heart failure and still chronically ill, the 86-year old Nobel laureate announced she will soon step down after 47 years as superior general of the Missionaries of Charity."[91]

The end came quietly for Mother Teresa on Friday, September 5, 1997. She died of heart failure at the motherhouse.

For the first hours after her death, her body rested in the motherhouse chapel. It

Why Was Sister Nirmala Chosen to Lead After Mother Teresa?

A few weeks after the Missionaries of Charity elected Sister Nirmala Joshi to take over as mother general of the order, the feature "Receiving the Torch," by Bruce Frankel, Jan McGirk, and Sarah Delaney, appeared in People *magazine.*

"Born in Bihar, the eldest of 10 children, Kusum Nirmala Joshi first encountered Christianity as a young child at a Carmelite boarding school 150 miles from her home. (Elite Hindu families traditionally send their daughters to convent schools to be educated.) In exchange for having the nuns teach Nirmala English and math, her father and her mother, Mohini, accepted that their daughter would be exposed to the Bible. But the slaughter, in the name of religion, of hundreds of thousands of Muslims and Hindus after Indian independence in 1947 horrified the 13-year-old girl and left her with a spiritual craving that slowly turned her toward Catholicism.

Witnessing a simple act of devotion proved a catalyst. One Sunday, when she was 17, as bells rang for morning chapel, Nirmala saw a classmate drop to her knees, eyes closed, crossing herself. '[And] at that moment, Jesus entered my heart,' Nirmala said recently, confiding, 'I had great problems accepting this religion. It took seven years for me to join.'

It was her worldliness rather than her contemplative nature that Mother Teresa first sought to make use of when Nirmala arrived at the Missionaries of Charity convent with a master's degree in political science. Soon, Mother Teresa sent her to law school so she could advise on adoption contracts and other legal matters. 'With Sister Nirmala, you feel the edge of an intellect,' says an Italian volunteer at the Home for the Destitute and Dying in Calcutta. 'If you speak to her, [she] is totally there.' . . .

When Mother Teresa was bedridden after a fall, Nirmala was assigned as her spiritual aide. Together the two planned the order's contemplative wing, emphasizing the mystical power of prayer. . . . 'She really is a person of prayer,' says Father Sebastian Vazhakala of the Brothers of the Missionaries of Charity in Rome. . . . 'Thanks to her steady hand, . . . the order will not die.'"

was then transferred to St. Thomas Church, Middleton Row, Calcutta, where mourners, two hundred thousand a day, from Calcutta and all over the world could pass by to pay their last respects.

FUNERAL IN CALCUTTA

On September 13, 1997, the open casket of Mother Teresa, decorated with symbols from her adopted country, India, was carried through the streets of Calcutta in an impressive funeral procession. Escorted by soldiers with red trim on their caps (signifying a state funeral), the casket rode the same gun carriage that had, in the past, transported the bodies of Mahatma Gandhi and Jawaharlal Nehru through the streets past thousands of mourners.

It was raining as people lined up seven deep along the route to the sports arena, Netaji Indoor Stadium, where a simple funeral mass was to be celebrated. In accordance with Indian funeral custom, many ran alongside the funeral cortege, trying to keep up with the honor guard. Many climbed trees or buildings to throw lotus blossoms.

Wives of dignitaries came from around the world: First Lady Hillary Rodham Clinton from the United States; Queen Sofia of Spain; Queen Fabiola of Belgium; Queen Noor of Jordan; Katharine, the

At the end of forty-seven years as superior general of the Missionaries of Charity, Mother Teresa blesses Sister Nirmala, the new leader of the order.

The funeral cortege of Mother Teresa makes its way past the crowds of people who have gathered to mourn the death of one who many revered as a living saint.

duchess of Kent, representing the royal family of England; and Bernadette Chirac, first lady of France. Most Reverend Angelo Sodano, the Vatican secretary of state, and Archbishop Henry D'Souza of Calcutta represented the highest offices of the Catholic Church. Mother Teresa's niece, Aggi Bojaxhiu Guttardo, came from Sicily.

In a tribute to Mother Teresa's simplicity and practicality, her grave marker, a large stone slab, lies in the motherhouse. The street that used to be called Lower Circular Road is now called A. J. C. Bose Road, but that place changes little. It is still a center of prayer, and Mother Teresa remains close to the people she served.

The Legacy

Continuation of cheerful and free service to the poorest of the poor, under the direction of Mother Teresa's successor, Sister Nirmala Joshi, seems assured, although a spiritual adviser to the order, Father C. Bouche, told Reuters News Service that the coming years would be "a period of consolidation for the order rather than growth."[92] In the tradition of their founder, the work goes on if the sisters remain poor and do not begin serving the rich.

Mary Poplin, a professor of education at the Claremont Graduate School in California, volunteered at the children's home in Calcutta in 1996. She writes of how the sisters, serving in a country that bears 21 percent of the global disease burden and a population that will pass a billion by the year 2000, are preserving the legacy of Mother Teresa:

> Each sister owns no more than what will fit into a small box. Each of them has three saris, one for special occasions, and two which are alternated; one is washed each day while the other is worn. Each of them has a prayer book and song book with covers made out of what appears to be brown paper bags—the books' pages

Under Sister Nirmala Joshi, the Missionaries of Charity will continue Mother Teresa's legacy.

typed on old manual typewriters—a Bible, a cup and dish, a pillow, pillow case and two sheets, a rosary, and a crucifix pin which holds the sari securely. The sisters eat like the poor. And like those they serve, they look forward to ice cream the day after Easter and the day after Christmas. . . .

It is important to understand that they do not embrace this hard life simply to better understand and serve the poor. Rather, they are poor in order to follow Christ, who chose to be poor, to be born in a stable, to live and die with no possessions.[93]

IMPORTANCE TO THE WORLD

Mother Teresa never intended to start a movement or establish a dynasty. She cared only that individuals cared for individuals, seeing their service as given to God. Eileen Egan, Mother Teresa's first biographer, puts Mother Teresa's importance to the world in these words in her tribute to her long-time friend:

What the world was responding to was a woman consumed by the Gospel of Jesus, a woman living out all the Beatitudes, but the very incarnation of one of them: "Blessed are the merciful." Mother Teresa took Jesus at his word and accepted him with unconditional love in those with whom he chose to be identified—the hungry, the shelterless, the suffering. She enveloped them in mercy. Mercy, after all, is only love

under the aspect of need, love going out to meet the needs of the person loved.[94]

Despite her fame, Mother Teresa adhered to her vow by remaining poor like the needy that she dedicated her life to serving.

ONE MIRACLE AFTER ANOTHER

The experience of Brother Tom Petitte in founding Lazarus House in Lawrence, Massachusetts, is an example of carrying Mother Teresa's mission home. Courtney Tower, in "Mother Teresa's Miracle of Grace," chronicles the success of this homegrown center of charity.

"'It's been one miracle after another,' says Brother Tom. 'We survive through the generosity of God's people, the grace and intervention of the Holy Spirit, and plain old hard work.'

What Brother Tom and the people of Lawrence have done serves as an example of what Co-Workers and followers of Mother Teresa do in many hundreds of towns and cities around the world. Today, Lazarus House shelters homeless people referred by Roman Catholicism, Greek Orthodox, Congregational, Lutheran and other churches and by social-service agencies. It feeds them and many others who come during the day seeking food. It helps them find a lodging, sometimes a job.

As in Mother Teresa's other houses, the holiness, says Brother Tom, 'works both ways—in our small staff and 70-odd volunteers and the hundreds who help out one way or another really feeling we serve Jesus in the poor.' Such love, grace and hard work serve over 13,000 meals in a year, fill up over 6,400 beds—under the eye of a 21-member board of all faiths. Activities begin and end with prayer. The services each week are inter-denominational and overflowing. Brother Tom, now age 42, still tramps the streets in his habit, walking under the Central bridge to find homeless outcasts huddled there and in abandoned cars and burned-out buildings, as he did to start Lazarus House."

A "MIRACLE" IN LAWRENCE, MASSACHUSETTS

The question is how the world will hear and respond to Mother Teresa's message.

How will the lives of people in the next millenium be changed? The answer may be found in the experience of one of Mother Teresa's volunteers, Brother Tom Petitte from Lawrence, Massachusetts. When he asked to stay in Calcutta at the end of a third summer with the missionaries in Calcutta, he was told by Mother Teresa to look at home for the poor. Brother Tom's response is narrated by Courtney Tower in "Mother Teresa's Miracle of Grace":

> "At first I was disappointed," Brother Tom says, but he returned to Lawrence, a mill town of 59,000, and found its hidden poor, people who "had been the working poor, and had fallen off the edge and become the very poor." Determined and eloquent, he sold Lawrence on the need for a temporary refuge for homeless people. Melchite Eastern rite Catholics raised $10,000 for the down payment on a 15-room Victorian home at 48 Holly Street. Service clubs donated money. Merchants and institutions gave food and materials. Carpenters, plumbers, electricians, volunteered to refurbish the building, and Lazarus House opened in the spring of 1983.[95]

Years before she died, Mother Teresa called attention to the paradox of being poor. Speaking with Edward W. Desmond of *Time*, she pointed out: "The less you have, the more free you are. . . . The rich are poorer than the poor: they are more lonely inside. They always need something more. . . . The hunger for love is much more difficult to remove than the hunger for bread."[96]

Notes

Introduction: Everyone's Peacemaker

1. Kathryn Spink, *Mother Teresa: A Complete Authorized Biography.* San Francisco: HarperSanFrancisco, 1997, p. xi.

2. Mother Teresa, *Words to Love By.* Notre Dame, IN: Ave Maria, 1983, p. 80.

Chapter 1: A Happy Family in the Eye of a Storm (1910–1928)

3. Quoted in Eileen Egan, *Such a Vision of the Street.* New York: Doubleday, 1985, p. 7.

4. Quoted in Egan, *Such a Vision of the Street,* p. 7.

5. Egan, *Such a Vision of the Street,* p. 8.

6. Egan, *Such a Vision of the Street,* p. 26.

7. Mother Teresa, *No Greater Love,* eds. Becky Benenate and Joseph Durepos. Novato, CA: New World Library, 1994, pp. 191–92.

8. Quoted in Malcolm Muggeridge, *Something Beautiful for God.* New York: Harper & Row, 1971, p. 83.

9. Quoted in Mother Teresa, *No Greater Love,* pp. 191–92.

10. Quoted in Egan, *Such a Vision of the Street,* p. 6.

11. Quoted in Egan, *Such a Vision of the Street,* p. 7.

12. Quoted in Egan, *Such a Vision of the Street,* p. 8.

13. Mother Teresa, *No Greater Love,* p. 146.

14. Mother Teresa, *No Greater Love,* pp. 1–2.

15. Quoted in Egan, *Such a Vision of the Street,* p. 13.

Chapter 2: Behind Cloister Walls in Calcutta (1928–1946)

16. Quoted in Lush Gjergji, *Mother Teresa: Her Life, Her Works,* trans. Richard Armandez.
New York: New City, 1991, p. 35.

17. Quoted in Gjergji, *Mother Teresa,* pp. 22–23.

18. Gjergji, *Mother Teresa,* p. 23.

19. Quoted in Gjergji, *Mother Teresa,* p. 25.

20. Quoted in Gjergji, *Mother Teresa,* p. 28.

21. Quoted in Egan, *Such a Vision of the Street,* p. 17.

22. Quoted in Gjergji, *Mother Teresa,* p. 29.

23. Quoted in Gjergji, *Mother Teresa,* p. 29.

24. Egan, *Such a Vision of the Street,* p. 19.

25. Mother Immolata Wetter, "School of Mary 1612," Archives of the Generalate of the Jesuits, Rome, n.d., p. 1.

26. Quoted in Gjergji, *Mother Teresa,* pp. 34–35.

27. Mother Teresa, *Words to Love By,* p. 21.

28. Quoted in Gjergji, *Mother Teresa,* p. 36.

29. Quoted in Gjergji, *Mother Teresa,* pp. 36–37.

30. Quoted in Egan, *Such a Vision of the Street,* p. 24.

31. Quoted in Egan, *Such a Vision of the Street,* p. 24.

32. Quoted in Egan, *Such a Vision of the Street,* p. 25.

Chapter 3: Testing a New Calling (1946–1960)

33. Quoted in Egan, *Such a Vision of the Street,* p. 33.

34. Quoted in Egan, *Such a Vision of the Street,* p. 34.

35. Navin Chawla, *Mother Teresa: The Authorized Biography.* Rockport, MA: Element, 1992, p. 35.

36. Quoted in Chawla, *Mother Teresa,* p. 37.

37. Quoted in Chawla, *Mother Teresa*, p. 38.

38. Quoted in Chawla, *Mother Teresa*, p. 46.

39. Quoted in Chawla, *Mother Teresa*, p. 48.

40. Quoted in Chawla, *Mother Teresa*, p. 54.

41. Quoted in Chawla, *Mother Teresa*, p. 57.

42. Quoted in Egan, *Such a Vision of the Street*, p. 42.

43. Quoted in Desmond Doig, *Mother Teresa: Her People and Her Work*. New York: Harper & Row/Nachiketa, 1976, p. 77.

44. Quoted in Chawla, *Mother Teresa*, p. 107.

45. Egan, *Such a Vision of the Street*, p. 319.

46. Quoted in Chawla, *Mother Teresa*, p. 108.

47. Quoted in Kathryn Spink, *Miracle of Love: Mother Teresa of Calcutta, Her Missionaries of Charity, and Her Co-Workers*. San Francisco: Harper & Row, 1981, p. 121.

Chapter 4: Expanding the Ministry to the Unwanted (1960–1970)

48. Quoted in Roger Marchand, *Mother Teresa of Calcutta: Her Life and Her Work*. Liguori, MO: Liguori, 1982, pp. 9–10.

49. Marchand, *Mother Teresa of Calcutta*, pp. 14–15.

50. Quoted in Spink, *Miracle of Love*, p. 89.

51. José Luis Gonzales-Baldado, *Mother Teresa, Her Life, Her Work, Her Message*. Liguori, MO: Liguori, 1997, p. 77.

52. Quoted in Gjergji, *Mother Teresa*, p. 76.

53. Quoted in Gjergji, *Mother Teresa*, p. 75.

54. Spink, *Miracle of Love*, p. 97.

Chapter 5: Boundary Crossings (1970–1979)

55. Quoted in Gjergji, *Mother Teresa*, p. 77.

56. Quoted in Gjergji, *Mother Teresa*, p. 78.

57. B. Srinivasa Murthy, *Mother Teresa and India*. Long Beach, CA: Long Beach, 1983, pp. 92, 96.

58. Quoted in Doig, *Mother Teresa*, p. 156.

59. Quoted in Chawla, *Mother Teresa*, p. 112.

60. Quoted in Spink, *Miracle of Love*, p. 82.

61. Quoted in Chawla, *Mother Teresa*, p. 177.

62. Quoted in Spink, *Mother Teresa*, p. 94.

63. Quoted in Doig, *Mother Teresa*, p. 23.

64. Quoted in Spink, *Mother Teresa*, p. 147.

65. Quoted in Spink, *Miracle of Love*, p. 110.

66. Mother Teresa, *A Simple Path*, comp. Lucinda Vardey. New York: Ballantine, 1995, p. 100.

67. Quoted in Egan, *Such a Vision of the Street*, p. 278.

68. Courtney Tower, "Mother Teresa's Work of Grace," *Reader's Digest*, December 1987, pp. 219–20.

Chapter 6: A Peacemaker Above Politics

69. Quoted in Chawla, *Mother Teresa*, p. 184.

70. Quoted in Gjergji, *Mother Teresa*, pp. 140–41.

71. Quoted in Robert Serrou, *Teresa of Calcutta: A Pictorial Biography*. New York: McGraw-Hill, 1980, p. 112.

72. Chawla, *Mother Teresa*, p. 189.

73. Quoted in Eileen Egan, "'Blessed Are the Merciful,'" *America*, September 20, 1997, p. 21.

74. Mother Teresa, *A Simple Path*, p. 133.

75. Peggy Noonan, "A Combatant in the World," *Time*, September 15, 1997, p. 84.

76. Stephanie Harrington, "Mother Teresa: The Last Obedient Woman," *Ms.*, March 1986, p. 98.

77. Quoted in Spink, *Mother Teresa*, p. 214.

78. Spink, *Mother Teresa*, p. 215.

79. Spink, *Mother Teresa*, p. 178.

80. Quoted in Spink, *Mother Teresa*, p. 213.

81. Quoted in Serrou, *Teresa of Calcutta*, p. 68.

Chapter 7: "She Was Tough" (1991–1997)

82. Quoted in Spink, *Mother Teresa,* pp. 255–56.

83. Spink, *Mother Teresa,* p. 257.

84. Noonan, "A Combatant in the World," p. 84.

85. Linda Schaefer, "Remembering Mother Teresa," *Catholic Digest,* August 1998, p. 22.

86. Michael Satchell, "Death Comes to a Living Saint," *U.S. News & World Report,* September 15, 1997, p. 12.

87. Christopher Hitchens, "Mother Teresa and Me," *Vanity Fair,* February 1995, pp. 37–38.

88. Hitchens, "Mother Teresa and Me," p. 43.

89. Marci McDonald, "Notes from a Spiritual Journey," *MacLean's,* December 25, 1996/January 1, 1997, p. 76.

90. Quoted in Spink, *Mother Teresa,* p. 269.

91. Dorian Friedman, "Taking a Much Deserved Rest," *U.S. News & World Report,* January 27, 1997, p. 18.

Epilogue: The Legacy

92. Quoted in *National Catholic Reporter,* "Sr. Nirmala Plans Travel, Invokes Guidance, Prayer," March 28, 1997, p. 7.

93. Mary Poplin, "No Humanitarian," *Commonweal,* December 19, 1997, p. 13.

94. Egan, "'Blessed Are the Merciful,'" p. 21.

95. Tower, "Mother Teresa's Miracle of Grace," p. 224.

96. Quoted in Edward W. Desmond, "A Pencil in the Hand of God," *Time,* December 4, 1989, p. 11.

For Further Reading

Books

Joan Graff Clucas, *Mother Teresa.* New York: Chelsea, 1988. A biography in the World Leaders Past and Present series. Several early photos.

Patricia Reilly Giff, *Mother Teresa, Sister to the Poor.* New York: Viking Kestrel and Puffin, 1986. Good historical background on the young Mother Teresa; watercolor illustrations.

William Jay Jacobs, *Mother Teresa: Helping the Poor.* Brookfield, CT: Millbrook, 1991. Descriptive biography for younger readers.

Linda Carlson Johnson, *Mother Teresa: Protector of the Sick.* Woodbridge, CT: Blackbirch, 1997. This biography gives good background and commentary on India.

Caroline Evensen Lazo, *Mother Teresa.* Parsippany, NJ: Dillon, 1993. A biography with considerable background and beautiful illustrations.

Claire Jordan Mohan, *The Young Life of Mother Teresa.* Worcester, PA: Young Sparrow, 1996. Written from a child's point of view with an appealing presentation.

Nina Morgan, *Mother Teresa, Saint of the Poor.* New York: Chelsea, 1988. Covers Mother Teresa's death; highly illustrated with bright color and sidebars.

Mildred M. Pond, *Mother Teresa: A Life of Charity.* New York: Chelsea, 1992. Opens with 1982 incident, then flashes back to early life. Some background.

Julina Popescu, *Let's Visit Yugoslavia.* London: Pegasus, 1984. A visitor's guide to Yugoslavia prior to the dissolution of the nation. Contains factual information on the areas where Mother Teresa lived as a youth.

Richard Tames, *Mother Teresa.* New York: Franklin Watts, 1989. An easy-to-read biography with sidebars and illustrations.

Mother Teresa, *Life in the Spirit.* New York: Harper & Row, 1983. Inspirational compilation of Mother Teresa's sayings.

———, *Mother Teresa: In My Own Words.* Liguori, MO: Liguori, 1997. More inspirational sayings from Mother Teresa.

———, *Words to Love By.* Notre Dame, IN: Ave Maria, 1983. Inspirations are categorized around issues of justice and prayer.

Periodicals

Sarah Gibbings, "Mother Teresa's Message to Diana," Inside Page/World Page Network, 1990. At age eighty, Mother Teresa tells Princess Diana her plans for a visit.

Mother Teresa, "I've Found God," *Saturday Evening Post*, July/August 1987. A brief photo feature on seeing God's face in the unwanted and suffering.

World Health, "Leaders in Health," April/May 1990. Mother Teresa is paneled with Dame Nita Barrow, representative to the United Nations, and Dame Cicely Saunders, founder of the hospice movement.

Works Consulted

Books

Joe David Brown and the Editors of Life, *India*. New York: Time, 1961. A history of India before Bangladesh independence.

Navin Chawla, *Mother Teresa: The Authorized Biography*. Rockport, MA: Element, 1992. Viewpoint of a Hindu doctor and businessman who visited Mother Teresa and interviewed many people from her early years in Calcutta.

Desmond Doig, *Mother Teresa: Her People and Her Work*. New York: Harper & Row/Nachiketa, 1976. Detailed interviews with missionaries and volunteers at work with the dying, lepers, and children.

Eileen Egan, *Such a Vision of the Street*. New York: Doubleday, 1985. Personalized biography by Mother Teresa's friend and confidant.

Lush Gjergji, *Mother Teresa: Her Life, Her Works*. Trans. Richard Armandez. New York: New City, 1991. Contains many quotations from Mother Teresa's early years and gives insights into her Catholic upbringing.

José Luis Gonzales-Baldado, *Mother Teresa, Her Life, Her Work, Her Message*. Liguori, MO: Liguori, 1997. Pays special attention to Mother Teresa's national and religious background. Sensitive to Catholic issues.

Dominique Lapierre, *City of Joy*. Trans. S. A. Pressinter. New York: Doubleday, 1985. Documents Catholic priest Stephen Kovalkski's ministry in Calcutta's slums and a meeting with Mother Teresa.

Lionel W. Lyde, *A Military Geography of the Balkan Peninsula*. London: Adam and Charles Black, 1905. Contains detailed information on the geography of Macedonia and adjoining countries.

Roger Marchand, *Mother Teresa of Calcutta: Her Life and Her Work*. Liguori, MO: Liguori, 1982. Brief biography of Mother Teresa that also contains insights on India.

Malcolm Muggeridge, *Something Beautiful for God*. New York: Harper & Row, 1971. Narration regarding the content of Muggeridge's film, including verbatim interviews conducted for this television documentary.

B. Srinivasa Murthy, *Mother Teresa and India*. Long Beach, CA: Long Beach, 1983. Helps to explain Mother Teresa's appeal in India.

V. V. Oak, *England's Educational Policy in India*. Madras, India: B. G. Paul, 1925. Study of Britain's schools in India, emphasizing missionary activities at some of the schools.

Robert Serrou, *Teresa of Calcutta: A Pictorial Biography*. New York: McGraw-Hill, 1980. Offers excellent historical background and illustrative material.

Kathryn Spink, *Miracle of Love: Mother Teresa of Calcutta, Her Missionaries of Charity, and Her Co-Workers.* San Francisco: Harper & Row, 1981. Contains especially detailed information on the Co-Workers. Many letters by Mother Teresa are reproduced and quoted in full.

———, *Mother Teresa: A Complete Authorized Biography.* San Francisco: HarperSanFrancisco, 1997. Some new material besides that involving the last years of Mother Teresa's life. Organized more by topic than chronology.

Edmund Stillman and the Editors of Life, *The Balkans.* New York: Time, 1964. Outlines the history and people of the Balkans to the time just before the Skopje earthquake.

Mother Teresa, *A Simple Path.* Comp. Lucinda Vardey. New York: Ballantine, 1995. Interviews with Mother Teresa and other Missionaries of Charity.

———, *No Greater Love.* Eds. Becky Benenate and Joseph Durepos. Novato, CA: New World Library, 1994. Inspirational messages of Mother Teresa.

Paul Theroux, *The Imperial Way: By Rail from Peshawar to Chittagong.* New York: Houghton-Mifflin, 1985. A description of India as experienced in a journey across the northern part of the country by a well-known travel writer.

Mark Tully and Zareer Masani, *Forty Years of Independence.* New York: George Braziller, 1988. A history of India from 1947 to 1987, emphasizing political aspects and personalities in Indian politics.

United Nations Development Programme, *Skopje Resurgent: The Story of a United Nations Special Fund Town Planning Project.* New York: United Nations, 1970. Maps and detailed plans of how the UN rebuilt Skopje after the 1963 earthquake.

Periodicals

Edward W. Desmond, "A Pencil in the Hand of God," *Time,* December 4, 1989.

N. S. Dharamshaktu, "Control Efforts in India," *World Health,* May/June 1996.

Eileen Egan, "'Blessed Are the Merciful,'" *America,* September 20, 1997.

Lawrence Eisenberg, "Deborah Raffin: My Visit with Mother Teresa," *Good Housekeeping,* April 1992.

Jeffrey Eugenides, "Compassionate Tourism," *New Yorker,* September 22, 1997.

Scott Farris, "A Lost Letter," *Catholic Digest,* November 1998.

Bruce Frankel and Jan McGirk, "A Last Goodbye," *People,* September 29, 1997.

———, "Receiving the Torch," *People,* June 30, 1997.

Dorian Friedman, "Taking a Much Deserved Rest," *U.S. News & World Report,* January 27, 1997.

Stephanie Harrington, "Mother Teresa: The Last Obedient Woman," *Ms.,* March 1986.

Christopher Hitchens, "Diana, Princess of Wales—Death and Burial; Mother Teresa—Death and Burial." *Nation,* September 29, 1997.

———, "Minority Report," *Nation,* April 13, 1992.

———, "Mother Teresa and Me," *Vanity Fair,* February 1995.

Philip K. Howard, "The Death of Common Sense," *U.S. News & World Report,* January 30, 1995.

Rita Koselka, "Connecting with Humanity," *Forbes,* November 3, 1997.

Sanjay Kumar, "Leprosy Vaccine Approved for Adjunctive Use in India," *Lancet,* February 14, 1998.

Amitabh Kundu, "Care for the Urban Poor," *World Health,* November/December 1994.

Dominique Lapierre, "Mother Teresa and the Leprosy of the Soul," *New Perspectives Quarterly,* Fall 1997.

Michel Lechat, "History of a Disease," *World Health,* May/June 1996.

Marci McDonald, "Notes from a Spiritual Journey," *MacLean's,* December 25, 1996/January 1, 1997.

Alan McGregor, "WHO Takes Aggressive Stance with Leprosy," *Lancet,* August 2, 1997.

National Catholic Reporter, "Sr. Nirmala Plans Travel, Invokes Guidance, Prayer," March 28, 1997.

———, "'Tiny Bit of Pencil' with Which God Wrote," September 19, 1997.

Peggy Noonan, "A Combatant in the World," *Time,* September 15, 1997.

Parabola, "Mother Teresa and the Poorest of the Poor," Spring 1991.

Mary Poplin, "No Humanitarian," *Commonweal,* December 19, 1997.

Reuters News Service, "A Saintly Nun and Her Chinese Host," *People Weekly,* February 11, 1985.

Francis Russell, "Mother Teresa at Harvard," *National Review,* July 23, 1982.

Michael Satchell, "Death Comes to a Living Saint," *U.S. News & World Report,* September 15, 1997.

Linda Schaefer, "Remembering Mother Teresa," *Catholic Digest,* August 1998.

Time, "For the Poor, an Immortal," September 22, 1997.

———, "Seeker of Souls," September 15, 1997.

Courtney Tower, "Mother Teresa's Work of Grace," *Reader's Digest,* December 1987.

Abraham Verghese, "Last Acts," *New Yorker,* September 22, 1997.

Mother Immolata Wetter, "School of Mary 1612," Archives of the Generalate of the Jesuits, Rome, n.d.

Joe Woodard, "A Hard and Happy Life," *Alberta Report/Western Report,* September 22, 1997.

———, "One Saint for the Puerile,

Another for the Poor," *Alberta Report/Western Report*, September 22, 1997.

————, "The Saint Who Cleaned Toilets," *Alberta Report/Western Report*, September 22, 1997.

Kenneth L. Woodward, "Requiem for a Saint," *Newsweek*, September 22, 1997

Index

Addis Ababa, Ethiopia, 73
Agnes, Sister, 43
    accompanies Mother
        Teresa to receive Nobel
        Peace Prize, 83
    on housing for
        Missionaries of
        Charity, 46
AIDS, 86, 88, 89
Albanian Catholic Choir of
    Skopje, 20
Albert Schweitzer
    International Prize, 78
Ali, Maula, 46
Andrew, Brother, 61
Antoni, Lorenc, 21
    on Mother Teresa's
        departure from Skopje,
        24
apartheid, 89

Balkan League, 14
Benitez, Bishop, 62
Bernard, Mother. See
    Xavier, Sister Francis
Bharat Ratna, 85
Blaikie, Anne, 50, 51
    Co-Workers of Mother
        Teresa and, 53, 76
    joins Missionaries of
        Charity, 52
    on Mother Teresa finding
        a novitiate, 64
Bojaxhiu, Aga (sister), 61,
    67, 68
    birth of, 13
    communication with
        Mother Teresa, 31, 61,
        67

joins Mother Teresa on
    journey to Ireland,
    23–25
Bojaxhiu, Agnes Gonxha.
    See Mother Teresa
Bojaxhiu, Dranafile
    (mother), 13, 14, 19
    charity work and , 16–17
    correspondence with
        Mother Teresa and, 31,
        32, 61
    on her daughter's
        decision to enter the
        Sisters of Loreto, 23
    after husband's death, 18
    joins Mother Teresa on
        journey to Ireland,
        23–25
    moves to live with Lazar,
        31
    pilgrimages of, 18
Bojaxhiu, Lazar (brother),
    14, 20, 51
    attends Nobel Peace
        Prize ceremony, 83
    birth of, 13
    on childhood of Mother
        Teresa, 15
    communication with
        Mother Teresa, 31, 51,
        61, 67
    Drana moves in with, 31
    on religion and his
        family, 18, 19
    reunited with Mother
        Teresa, 93
Bojaxhiu, Nikola (father),
    13, 14
    charity work and, 16–17

death of, 17
    political involvement of,
        17
Bouche, Father C., 106
Breen, Sister M. Thérêse 26
Brown, Jerry
    volunteers at Kalighat, 87
Bush, George, 86

Cambridge University, 80
Carmeline, Sister, 94
Carmichael Hospital for
    Tropical Diseases, 50
Catholic Missions, 24–25
    on Mother Teresa's first
        impressions of India,
        27
    on Mother Teresa
        working at hospital in
        Bengal, 28
Catholic Relief Services, 53,
    66
Catholic University of
    America, 71
Catholic Welfare Bureau,
    90
Chawla, Navin, 46
Chirac, Bernadette (first
    lady of France), 105
City of Joy (Lapierre)
    on founding of Nirmal
        Hriday, 48
    on mobile unit to serve
        leprosy victims, 91
Claremont Graduate
    School, 101, 106
Clinton, Hillary Rodham,
    104
Commonweal, 101

Congregation of Sisters of the Blessed Virgin Mary of Loreto. *See* Sisters of Our Lady of Loreto

Co-Workers of Mother Teresa, 72, 76
creation of, 53
dissolves as organization, 102

Das, Subhasini. *See* Agnes, Sister

Daughters of St. Anne, 30
Mother Teresa in charge of, 32, 34, 37

deDecker, Jacqueline, 50, 52, 72
attends Nobel Peace Prize ceremony, 83
creation of Links for Sick and Suffering Co-Workers and, 50–51
relationship with Mother Teresa, 51

de Gaulle, Charles, 68
Delaney, Sarah, 103
Desmond, Edward W., 109
Diana, Princess, 98
Doig, Desmond, 74
on converting, 69
on the leper ministry, 58
on living in the convent, 44
on Mother Teresa and St. Mary students, 42

Dolores, Sister, 79
Dorcic, Monsignor, 64
Dostoyevsky, Fyodor, 20
D'Souza, Archbishop Henry, 105
Duvalier, "Baby Doc", 94
Duvalier, Michele, 100

Egan, Eileen, 14, 50, 51, 53, 107
accompanies Mother Teresa to receive Nobel Peace Prize, 83
on Bojaxhiu family's charity work, 17
helps Mother Teresa visit family, 61
on Mother Teresa as a teacher at St. Mary's School, 29–30
on the Sisters of Loreto, 33
visits Rome with Mother Teresa, 65, 68

Fabiola (queen of Belgium), 104
FAO Ceres Medal, 78
Feast of Assumption of Mary, 22
Ferdinand, Archduke Francis, 15
First Balkan War, 14
Florence, Sister, 42, 71
Frankel, Bruce, 103
Frederica, Sister, 73

Gandhi, Indira, 68, 72
Gandhi, Mahatma, 32, 104
Mother Teresa compared to, 86
Gandhiji Prem Nivas, 60, 61
Geoff, Brother
on comparison between Western and Eastern views of time, 95
Gertrude, Sister
accompanies Mother Teresa to receive Nobel Peace Prize, 83
Gift of Love, 86

Gift of Mary, 93
Gjergji, Lush
on Drana moving to live with Lazar, 31
helps Mother Teresa visit family, 61
on Mother Teresa's childhood, 15
on Mother Teresa's first impressions of India, 27
on Mother Teresa's last night in Skopje, 23, 24
on Mother Teresa teaching at St. Teresa's Primary School, 29

Gomes, Alfred, 45
provides home for Mother Teresa, 41
Gomes, Magdalena, 43
Gomes, Michael, 45
provides home for Mother Teresa, 41
Good Housekeeping magazine, 96
Good Samaritan Award, 71
Good Shepherd Sisters, 34
Guttardo, Aggi Bojaxhiu, 105

Harrington, Stephanie, 88
on contradictions of Mother Teresa, 89
Hell's Angel (documentary), 100, 102
Henry, Father Julian, 32, 40
creation of a men's order and, 59
finds home for Mother Teresa, 41
Hitchens, Christopher, 100
Holy Family Hospital (Patna), 38

Home for the Destitute and
Dying, 103
Howrah Station, 45, 59

Ingendaa, Sister Stephanie
on her relationship with
Mother Teresa, 39
Institute of the Blessed
Virgin Mary, 22
Irwin, Mother M. Borgia, 25

Jambrenovic, Father
Franjo, 21, 23
establishes library at
Sacred Heart Church,
20
starts Sodality of the
Blessed Virgin Mary,
20
Jawaharlal Nehru Award,
71
John F. Kennedy
International Award, 71
José, Charmain
on Missionaries of
Charity work, 11
Joshi, Sister Nirmala, 103

Kajnc, Betika. See
Magdalene, Sister Mary
Katharine (duchess of
Kent), 105
Keating, Charles, 101
Kennedy, John F., 68
Kennedy, Mother Gertrude
M.
Mother Teresa's request
for exclaustration and,
37–38
Kovalski, Stephan, 91
Knox, Archbishop James
Robert, 53
Kurti, Father Stephan, 68

Lapierre, Dominique
on founding of Nirmal
Hriday, 48
on mobile unit to serve
leprosy victims, 91
Lazarus House, 108
leprosy, 55, 86, 96
Gandhiji Prem Nivas
and, 56–57, 60
mobile clinic and, 50, 53,
58
Life magazine
on Jerry Brown
volunteering at
Kalighat, 87
Lincoln Savings and Loan,
101
Links for Sick and
Suffering Co-Workers,
51, 52
Little Sisters of the Poor, 40
Loreto Abbey, 25
Loreto College. See
University College for
Women
Loreto Entally, 31, 32, 34,
37
becomes a military
hospital during World
War II, 34
Mother Teresa leaves, 35
Loreto House
in Auteuil, 25
in Calcutta, 25, 29, 33
in Rathfarnham, 25, 37

MacAvin, Mother Eugene,
25
Madonna of Letnice, 18
Mother Teresa visits, 22,
64
Magdalene, Sister Mary, 25

Magnificent Lotus Award
(the Padmashree), 56
Magsaysay Award, 57
Malfatto, Angelo, 93
Marchand, Roger, 54
on Hindu concept of
suffering, 55
Marcos, Ferdinand, 94
Maryknoll Sisters, 34
Mary of the Cenacle,
Mother, 31
Mater et Magistra Award,
71
McDonald, Marci, 102
McGirk, Jan, 103
Medal of Freedom, 88
Medical College Hospital,
48
Medical Mission Sisters, 38
Miracle of Love
on mission in Ireland, 72
Missionaries of Charity,
Contemplative, 80
Missionary Brothers of
Charity, 75, 95, 103
creation of, 59
mission to Vietnam, 76
Mother Teresa
on abortion, 84–85, 92
AIDS and, 86, 88, 89
on birth control, 84–85,
92
childhood of, 14, 15
decides to enter the
Sisters of Our Lady
of Loreto, 22, 23
high school years of,
20
interest in India, 21
interest in reading, 20
pilgrimages to
Madonna of Letnice,
22

poor health during, 18
communication with
family, 31–32, 61
Lazar and, 51, 67
compared to Mahatma
Gandhi, 86
death of, 102, 104
health of, 81–82, 97–98
India and
first impressions of, 27
journey to, 23–25
at Loreto novitiate,
25–26, 27
becomes Mother
Teresa, 31
becomes Sister Teresa,
25
Daughters of St. Anne
and, 30
in charge of, 32, 34, 37
leaves, 35
requests
exclaustration, 37–38
Sodality of the Blessed
Virgin Mary and, 32
teaches at St. Mary's
School, 29, 31–32, 34,
42
in charge of, 30
teaches at St. Teresa's
Primary School, 28,
29
and Missionaries of
Charity
Co-Workers of Mother
Teresa and, 53, 72, 76
dissolves as
organization, 102
creation of, 45
housing for, 46
leprosy and, 55, 86, 96
Gandhiji Prem Nivas
and, 56–57, 60

mobile clinic for, 48,
50, 53, 58, 91
Links for the Sick and
Suffering Co-
Workers and, 51, 52
Missionary Brothers of
Charity and, 59, 75,
95, 103
Nirmal Hriday and, 79
founding of, 47, 48,
91
Pope John Paul II
visits, 92
pilgrimage to Madonna
of Letnice, 64
receives awards and
honors, 71, 78, 80, 85, 88
Nobel Peace Prize, 82,
83–85
receives second call from
God, 34–35
trains with the Medical
Mission Sisters, 39
use of public attention,
10
visits Rome, 65, 68
Mother Teresa: A Complete
Authorized Biography
(Spink), 52
Mother Teresa: The
Authorized Biography
(Chawla), 46
Mother Teresa: Her Life, Her
Works (Gjergji)
on Drana's move to
Tirane, 31
on Mother Teresa's
childhood, 15
on Mother Teresa's first
impressions of India,
27
on Mother Teresa's last
night in Skopje, 24

on Mother Teresa teaching
at St. Teresa's Primary
School, 29
Mother Teresa: Her People
and Her Work (Doig)
on the leper ministry, 58
on living in the convent,
44
on Mother Teresa and St.
Mary students, 42
Mother Teresa of Calcutta:
Her Life and Her Work
(Marchand), 55
"Mother Teresa's Miracle
of Grace,"64, 108, 109
Moti Jihl, 32, 53
Ms. magazine, 88, 96
Muggeridge, Malcolm
on Mother Teresa and
Indian lepers, 55
Mullan, Hugh, 72
Murthy, B. Srinivasa, 69

Nation magazine, 100
National Catholic
Development
Conference, 71
Nehru, Jawaharlal (prime
minister), 54, 56, 104
Netaji Indoor Stadium, 104
Nero (Roman emperor), 20
Newsweek magazine, 96
Nilratan Sarrkar Hospital,
32
Nirmal Hriday, 79
founding of, 47, 48, 91
Pope John Paul II visits,
92
Nirmala Kennedy Centre,
71
Nobel Peace Prize, 10, 11,
82
ceremony and Mother

Teresa, 83, 85, 86
Noonan, Peggy, 88, 96
Noor (queen of Jordan),
    105
Norwegian Nobel
    Committee, 83

O'Connor, Cardinal John, 86

Park Circus (parish), 41
Patna Sisters, 41
Peace Corps, 10
People (magazine), 103
Perier, Archbishop
    Ferdinand, 21, 37, 41, 45
Petitte, Brother Tom, 108,
    109
Philip (prince of Britain),
    80
Pontifical Society for the
    Propagation of the Faith,
    24
Pope John Paul II
    visits India, 92
Pope John XXIII, 53
Pope John XXIII Peace
    Prize, 71
Pope Paul VI, 63, 92
    gives Mother Teresa his
        limousine, 57
    gives Pope John XXIII
        Peace Prize to Mother
        Teresa, 71
Poplin, Mary, 101
Princip, Gavrilo, 15

Quo Vadis? (Sienkiewicz), 20

Reagan, Ronald, 86
"Receiving the Torch"
    (Frankel), 103
Red Cross, 10, 64
Reddy, N. Sanjiva, 85

Reuters News Service, 106
Roy, R. C., 45
Rozario, Sister Bernard, 44,
    49
    on the leper ministry, 58

Sacred Heart of Jesus
    Church
    Bojaxhiu family and, 13,
        16, 18
    Mother Teresa and, 20, 22
Saint Anthony of Padua
    (parish), 80
Saint Joseph College, 27
Saint Joseph's Home, 40
Saint Mary's School, 29, 31,
    32, 34, 37
    students and Mother
        Teresa, 42
Saint Teresa's Primary
    School, 28, 29
    enclosure rule and, 30–31
Saint Thomas Church, 104
Sannes, John, 83
Satchell, Michael, 98
Schaefer, Linda, 97
Second Balkan War, 14
Second Vatican Council, 62
Selassie, Haile (emperor of
    Ethiopia), 73
Sen, P. C., 50, 55
Serrou, Robert, 19, 93
Shantinagar (village), 59, 71
Shishu Bhavan, 49, 53, 97
Sienkiewicz, Henryk, 20
Sierra Leone, 12
Simple Path, A (Vardey), 77,
    102
    on comparison between
        Western and Eastern
        views of time, 95
    on the leper ministry, 60
    on Missionaries of

Charity work, 11
    on Nirmal Hriday, 79
    on teaching volunteers, 81
Sisters of Our Lady of
    Loreto, 25, 72
    Mother Teresa decides to
        join, 22, 23
Skopje, 18, 20, 31
    history of, 13
        First Balkan War and,
            14
        Second Balkan War
            and, 15
        Treaty of Versailles
            and, 15–16
        World War I and, 15
    Mother Teresa's last
        night in, 23
    Mother Teresa returns to,
        64
Skopje Theater, 14
Sodality of the Blessed
    Virgin Mary, 20
    Mother Teresa as
        moderator of, 32
Sodano, Angelo (Vatican
    secretary of state), 105
Sofia (queen of Spain), 104
Something Beautiful for
    God (video)
    on Mother Teresa and
        Indian lepers, 55
Spink, Kathryn, 10, 52, 61
    on mission in Ireland, 72
    on Mother Teresa in
        South Africa, 89–90
    on Pope John Paul II's
        visit to India, 92
Such a Vision of the Street
    (Egan), 68
    on the Loreto Sisters, 33
Swedish Academy, 11
Templeton Award for

Progress in Religion, 71
Teresa, Mother. *See* Mother
   Teresa
Teresa of Calcutta (Serrou),
   19, 93
Thant, U., 68
Third Order of St. Francis,
   71
Time magazine, 88, 96, 109
Tower, Courtney, 108, 109
   on Mother Teresa finding
      a possible novitiate, 64
Travels-Ball, Ian, 59
Treaty of Bucharest, 14–15
Treaty of Versailles, 15–16
Tutu, Archbishop
   Desmond, 90

Udovc, Janez, 28
United Nations, 10, 66, 68
   Food and Agriculture
      Organization presents
      award to Mother
      Teresa, 78
University College for

Women, 33, 40
University of North
   Carolina, 78
University of Santiniketan-
   Visva-Bharati, 78
U.S. News & World Report
   magazine, 98, 102

Van Exem, Father Celeste,
   41, 45, 57
   creation of a men's order
      and, 59
   finds food for the sisters,
      44–45
   finds home for Mother
      Teresa, 41
   on housing for the
      Missionaries of
      Charity, 46
   as Mother Teresa's
      spiritual director, 37, 40
Vanity Fair magazine, 100
Vardey, Lucinda, 11, 102
   on comparison between
      Western and Eastern

      views of time, 95
   on the leper ministry, 60
   on Missionaries of
      Charity work, 11
   on Nirmal Hriday, 79
   on teaching new
      volunteers, 81
Vatican City, 93
Vazhakala, Father
   Sebastian, 103
Vincent, Agnes. *See*
   Florence, Sister
Viniod, Brother, 60

Ward, Mary, 30
World Health
   Organization, 50
World War I, 15
World War II, 51
   end of, 34
   India and, 32
Wynen, Sister Elise, 39

Xavier, Sister Francis, 45,
   59, 71

Picture Credits

Cover photo: © Raghu Rai/Magnum Photos, Inc.

AP/Wide World Photos, 40, 48, 49, 70, 75, 85, 88, 90, 92, 94, 98, 100, 107

Archive Photos, 20, 72, 74, 86

Archive Photos/Camera Press, 10, 39

Archive Photos/David Lees, 57

Archive Photos/Popperfoto, 63, 69

Corbis/Agence France Presse, 106

Corbis/Alison Wright, 47, 79

Corbis/Annie Griffiths Belt, 11

Corbis/Bettman-UPI, 67, 78, 80, 84, 87, 89

Corbis/Brian Vikander, 36

Corbis/David Cumming; Eye Ubiquitous, 56

Corbis/Earl Kowall, 26

Corbis/E.O. Hoppé, 21

Corbis/Hulton-Deutsch Collection, 27, 35, 38

Corbis/Nazima Kowall, 30, 33, 43, 62

Corbis/Paul Almasy, 13

Corbis/Zen Icknow, 50

Express Newspapers/Archive Photos, 73

Illustrated London News/Archive Photos, 16

Reuters/Andrew Wong/Archive Photos, 105

Reuters/Jayanta Shaw/Archive Photos, 104

Reuters/Mike Segar/Archive Photos, 99

About the Author

Rafael Tilton is an educator, editor and writer who has written four other books for young people. Tilton's interest in Catholic tradition and practice is grounded by membership in a religious community and lifelong promotion of human rights and social justice. After reading works by Nobel Prize–winner Sir Rabindranath Tagore and novelist Rumer Godden, Tilton found family members and friends who had spent extended periods of time in India. Their first-hand accounts brought a personal dimension to this study of Mother Teresa of Calcutta.